Walla Walla Valley MEMORIES

THE EARLY YEARS

PRESENTED BY

WALLA WALLA UNION-BULLETIN
We Bring the Valley Home to You

Acknowledgements

The Walla Walla Union-Bulletin and Fort Walla Walla Museum are pleased to present "Walla Walla Valley Memories: The Early Years." This unique pictorial book is not a publication of just these two entities, however. It is the result of contributions made by many people from throughout the Walla Walla Valley.

We are indebted, first of all, to those early Valley residents who captured their time—our history—in photographs, and provided us with a glimpse into their lives. And, secondly, all Valley residents are indebted to the organizations and individuals who are committed to preserving our history in archives and personal collections.

In addition to the generous contributions of both time and photo archives from Fort Walla Walla Museum, we also received valuable assistance from the numerous Union-Bulletin readers who took the time to share their photos and stories. We would like to specifically thank Fred L. Mitchell, who shared generously from his extensive private collection of historic images.

We also thank the talented individuals who provided invaluable assistance in correcting and expanding the captions in this book, including: Paul Franzmann and Laura Schulz both from Fort Walla Walla Museum; Dan Clark, Larry Dodd, and Mary Meeker of the Historic Resources Coordinating Committee; and Doug Saturno of The Clock Shop and Antique Company, Walla Walla.

Copyright© 2006 The Union-Bulletin • ISBN: 1-59725-078-3

All rights reserved. No part of this book may be reproduced, stored in a retrieval system or transmitted in any form or by any means, electronic, mechanical, photocopying, recording or otherwise, without prior written permission of the copyright owner or the publisher.
Published by Pediment Publishing, a division of The Pediment Group, Inc. www.pediment.com Printed in the Canada

Contents

Foreword 5

Views Around the Valley 7

Working the Land 19

Transportation 33

Commerce & Industry 43

Schools & Education 63

Tradition of Public Service 85

People of the Valley 99

Disaster Strikes 125

Recreation & Celebration 135

Foreword

The Walla Walla Valley has long been recognized as the cradle of Northwest history. During their time in this area, Lewis and Clark traveled through the homelands of the Palouse, Walla Walla, and Cayuse Tribes. The Oregon Trail branched through here with travelers stopping by the Whitman Mission. Men working the Idaho mines would venture to the area for supplies. For awhile there was talk of the state capital being located here – not so far fetched when you consider this was the home of the last territorial governor and one of the largest and most prosperous cities in the territory at the time.

This book is dedicated to all those individuals who helped shape the Walla Walla Valley into the area we love so dearly today. It is not meant as a definitive history book and does not attempt to cover all possible events. The photographs will take you on a visual journey through the area from the later part of the 1800s to 1939. You will watch the growth of towns and areas – such as Walla Walla, College Place, Dayton, Waitsburg, Lowden, Prescott, Starbuck, Wallula, Touchet, Huntsville, Burbank, Milton-Freewater, Weston and Athena – and see changes in agriculture, transportation, businesses and schools. Dozens of local residents have shared treasured family pictures and Fort Walla Walla Museum has generously shared photographs to help you take a step back in time. Many of these photographs have never been published until now.

Accuracy is an important factor in publishing a historical book. The owners of the pictures supplied information about the photographs. Efforts have been made to verify locations, dates, names and spellings. Special thanks go to Larry Dodd, Mary Meeker, Dan Clark and James Payne for their efforts. If you have additional information about anything in this book or if you have historical photos you would like to donate to Fort Walla Walla Museum for preservation and display, please contact Fort Walla Walla Museum. Publication of historic photographs can be aided by making sure everyone in the picture is identified. If you have collections of family photos, do future generations a big favor and take the time to identify people and dates. Today's pictures are tomorrow's history.

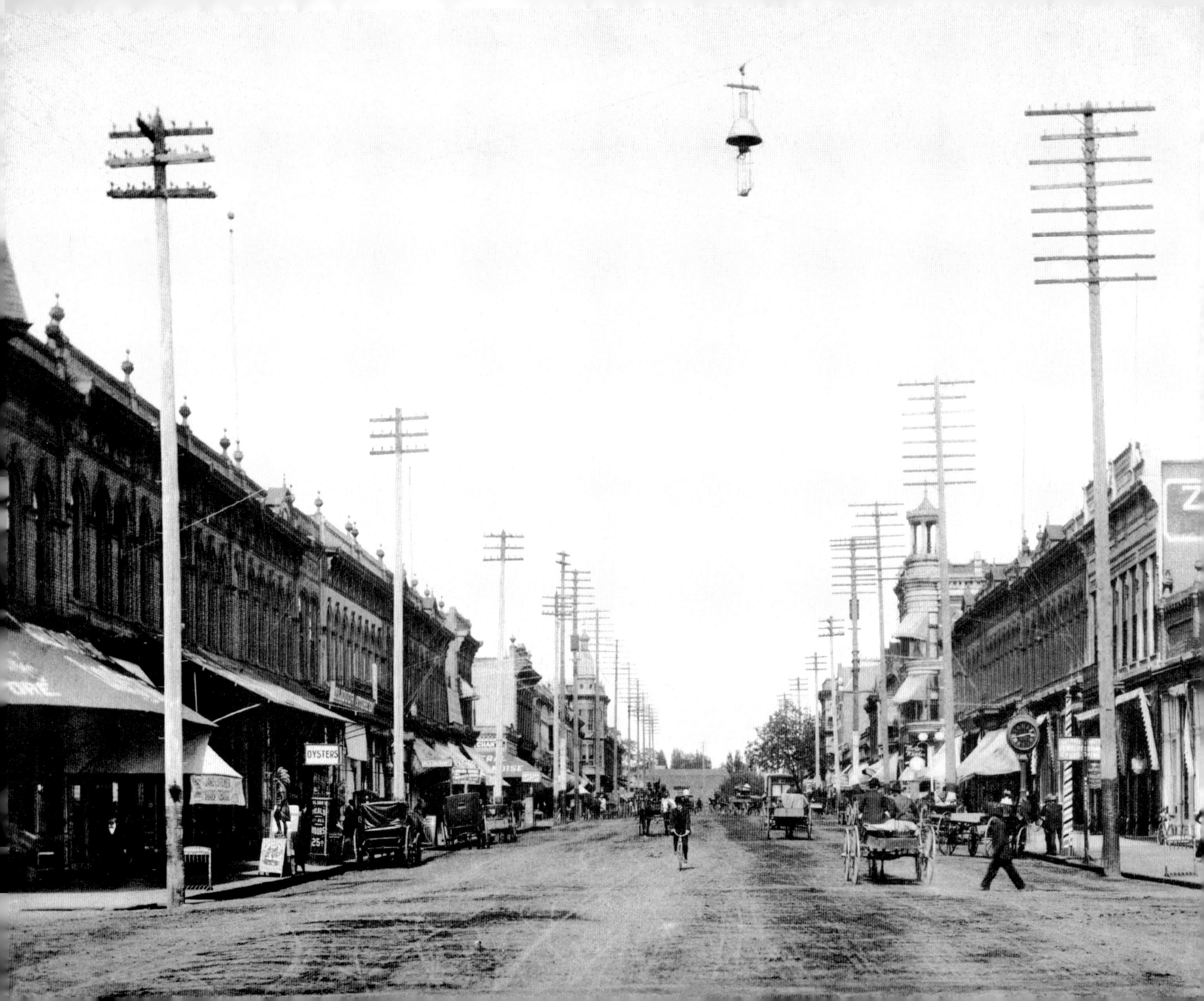
OYSTERS

CHAPTER ONE
Views Around the Valley

Main Street. Every town has one and every Main Street has a story to tell. Early street scenes in area towns show wooden structures, dirt streets, horses and buggies. Photographs taken from high above show the growth from rural gathering places to vital centers of economic activity. Homes and businesses branch off Main Street like spider webs. Before long, brick buildings with impressive architecture, paved streets, early models of cars and streetcars spring up throughout the downtown areas. Electric and telephone lines attest to the changing times and technologies.

Much of the Valley's early history still remains. Buildings that captivated attention at the end of the 19th century and early in the 20th century are still found up and down streets in area towns. Streetcar tracks can still be seen embedded in some streets. But there are also the structures, grand in their time, that have disappeared except in photographs such as these.

Left: A view of Main Street, looking east from 4th Street in Walla Walla, circa 1900. The three-story cupola at left is the Rees-Winans Building on 2nd Street. *Photo courtesy Francis Christiano*

Right: An early view of Main Street in Walla Walla, looking west from 1st Street with the bridge over Mill Creek in the foreground, circa 1875. *Photo courtesy Francis Christiano*

Above: A bird's eye view of the Whitman Eells Memorial Church and the mission grounds behind the church, looking west, circa 1890.
Photo courtesy Fort Walla Walla Museum #UK.UK.7328

Left: Horse show on Main Street, Dayton, early 1900s.
Photo courtesy Fort Walla Walla Museum #UK.UK.7433B

Above: Buildings along South 2nd Street in Walla Walla, late 1800s. The two-story brick building is the John Stahl house. The City Brewery, built by Stahl in 1880 is at right. *Photo courtesy Fort Walla Walla Museum #94.9.24*

Right: Looking east on Main Street, at or near 5th Street, Walla Walla, circa 1900. *Photo courtesy Fort Walla Walla Museum #93.137.5*

Views Around the Valley

Above: An early view of the south side of Main Street in Walla Walla, east of 2nd street, circa 1890.
Photo courtesy Tracy Cornell

Above left: Looking east on Main Street, east of 4th Street, Walla Walla, circa 1905.
Photo courtesy Fort Walla Walla Museum #06.24.2

Left: Bird's eye view of Prescott, circa 1905.
Photo courtesy Fort Walla Walla Museum #92.69.4

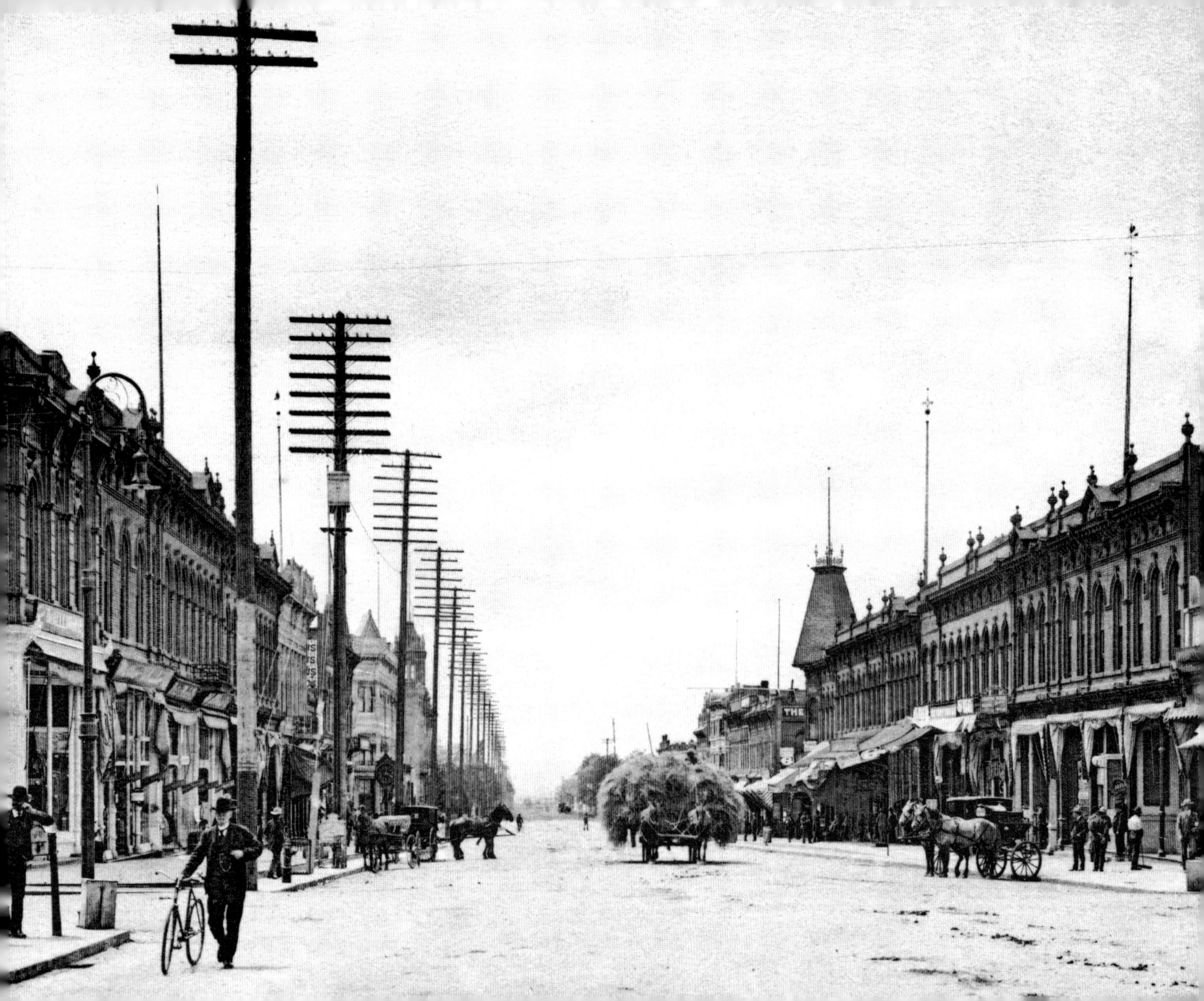

Above: A view of Alder Street, looking west from 1st Street, Walla Walla, circa 1905. The Golden Rule Building—later the Grand Hotel—is on the right. *Photo courtesy Fort Walla Walla Museum #06.24.2*

Left: Main Street in Walla Walla, looking east from 6th Street, circa 1900. The courthouse is at right. *Photo courtesy Fort Walla Walla Museum #95.42.28*

Far Left: A view of Main Street, looking west from 3rd Street, Walla Walla, circa 1905. *Photo courtesy Fort Walla Walla Museum #06.24.2*

11

Right: View of Main Street from Palouse Street looking west, circa 1917. The Walla Walla Hotel is on the left. Dahlen Auto Co., built in 1917, is at right.

Photo courtesy Fred L. Mitchell

Above: A view of Lowden, circa 1906. *Photo courtesy Larry Dodd*

Right: A view of Main Street, looking east from 5th Street, circa 1905. The I.O.O.F. Lodge building is at right.

Photo courtesy Virgil Reynolds

Views Around the Valley

Left: A view of Main Street in Walla Walla from 1st Street, looking west, circa 1910.
Photo courtesy Virgil Reynolds

Below left: Main Street in Walla Walla, circa 1912. This view is from between Palouse and Spokane streets.
Photo courtesy Fred L. Mitchell

Below: A view of Starbuck from the southwest, circa 1911.
Photo courtesy Tina (Clodius) Allington

Right: A view of the north side of Alder Street in Walla Walla, from mid-block between Colville and 1st streets, looking west, circa 1914.
Photo courtesy Virgil Reynolds

Above: Main Street from First Street looking west, Walla Walla, circa 1914.
Photo courtesy Fred L. Mitchell

Right: A bird's eye view of Walla Walla in 1913, looking east above Rose and 6th streets.
Photo courtesy Virgil Reynolds

Far right: A view of Main Street, Walla Walla, looking west, circa 1914.

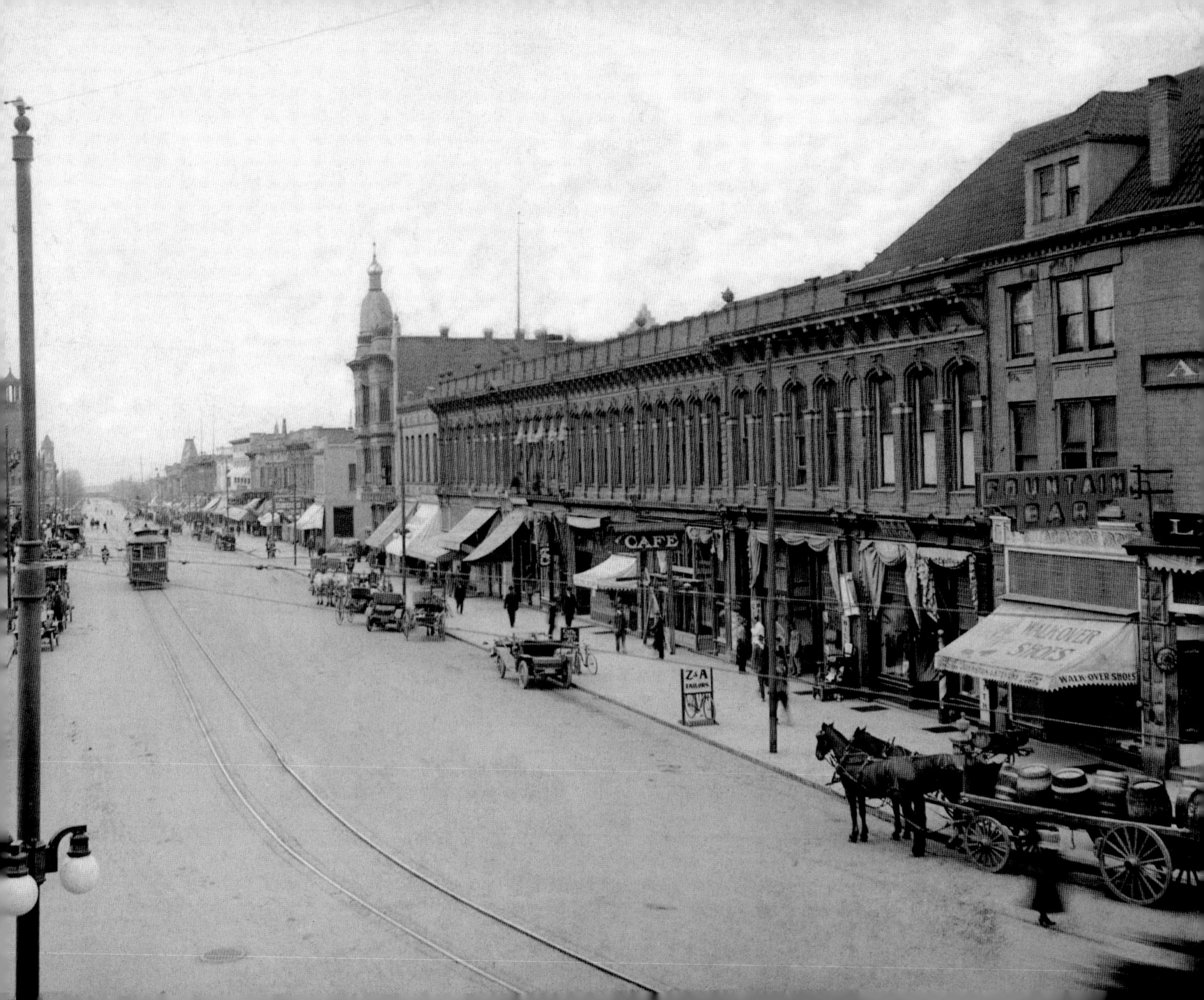
CAFE
FOUNTAIN
WALKOVER SHOES
WALK-OVER SHOES
Z&A TAILORS

Above: First and Main streets, looking west, Walla Walla, decorated for the rodeo, circa 1939. *Photo courtesy Fort Walla Walla Museum #87.62.4*

Right: A bird's eye view looking west down Main Street in Walla Walla, from the Baker Boyer Bank Building at 2nd Street, circa 1915. *Photo courtesy Virgil Reynolds*

Top: Panoramic view of the southeast corner of 1st and Main streets in Walla Walla, circa 1915. *Photo courtesy Daryl Foster*

Views Around the Valley

Above: Main Street, looking west from the Die Brücke Building at 1st Street, Walla Walla, 1927. *Photo courtesy Fred L. Mitchell*

Left: Looking north on College Avenue from 4th Street in College Place, circa 1939. *Photo courtesy Fort Walla Walla Museum #05.2.10*

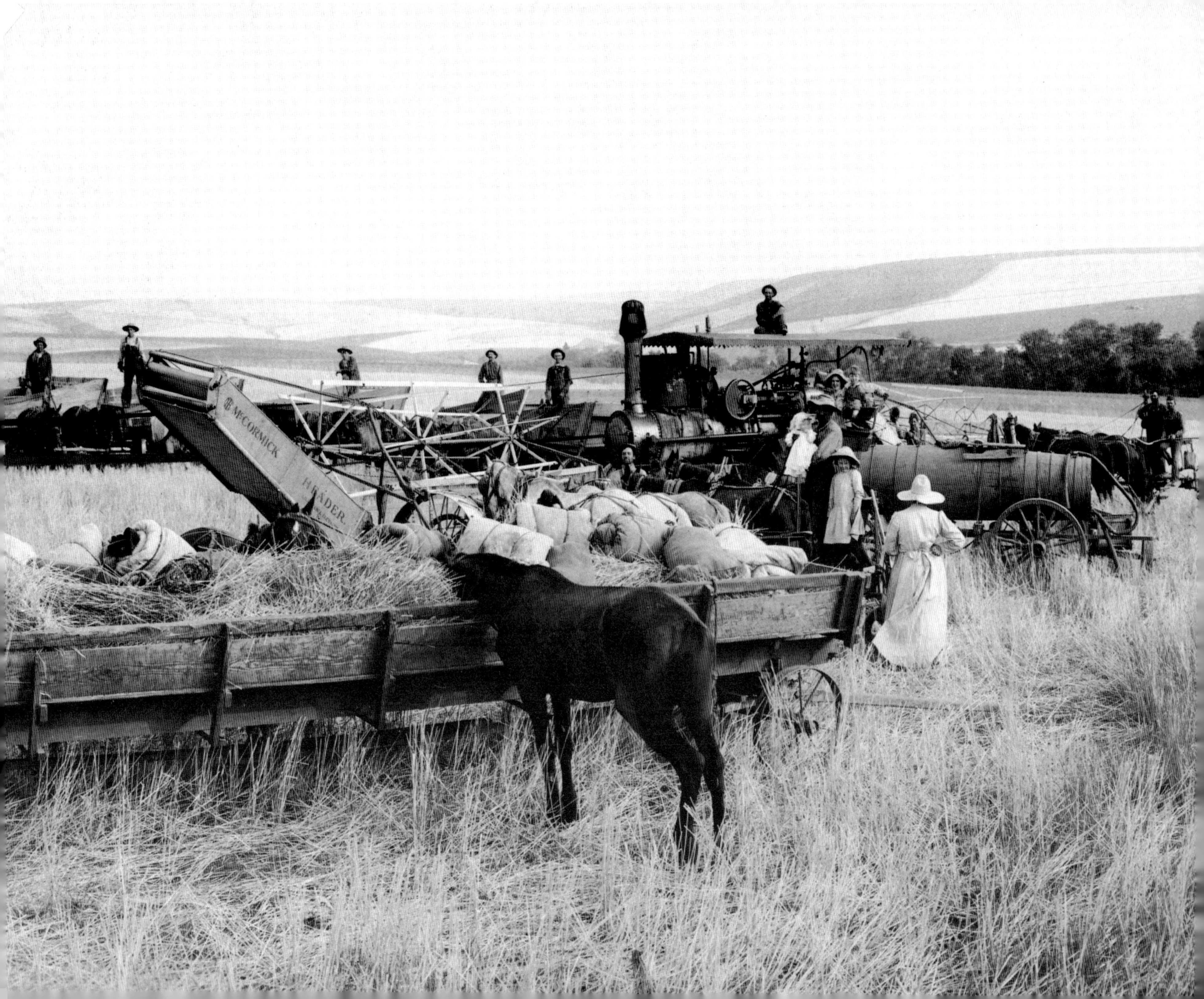
McCORMICK

CHAPTER TWO
Working the Land

Agriculture has always been one of the major foundations of the local economy. Wheat may have been king, but the Walla Walla Valley has seen many different agricultural crops and livestock thrive. Orchards and onions have a long, successful history in the area. And sheep proved to be a way to spread risk by providing two marketable products: wool and meat. If demand was low for one, there was always the opportunity to cash in on the other.

The rolling hills of the area presented challenges for planting and for harvesting. The use of teams of mules or horses hitched to wheat combines with special devices to keep the machinery level opened land that otherwise would have been impossible to cultivate.

Even with technological innovations, the backbone of agriculture was still the workers. It took large crews exerting a lot of manual labor to bring in the wheat, fruit and other crops. Feeding these crews usually required the combined efforts of the women of the farms and sometimes involved using horses or mules to pull large cookhouses into the fields.

Left: Scene in Athena, Oregon area of the Ringel and Bannister harvest, 1912. Included in this scene are five header boxes with drivers, two push headers, a water wagon, and steam engine. *Photo courtesy Fort Walla Walla Museum #92.130.3B*

Right: Farm workers standing beside a steam engine, circa 1900.
Photo courtesy Fort Walla Walla Museum #UK.24.4

Above: Harvesting scene on the Kennedy Farm, Walla Walla area, early 1900s.
Photo courtesy Douglas Saturno

Left: Horse-drawn farming equipment in the Walla Walla area, early 1900s.
Photo courtesy Fred L. Mitchell

Above: W.H. Berney Fruit Farm, Walla Walla, circa 1900.
Photo courtesy Fort Walla Walla Museum #02.1.79

Right: The farm of Civil War veteran Silas H. Timmons, located five miles west of Walla Walla on Wallula Road, circa 1895. Timmons' son, John H. Timmons, is on the horse at right. *Photo courtesy Susan Queen*

Above: A stationery threshing crew on the Ringel and Bannister operation. The men are sitting on sacks of grain in a cut wheat field. In the front row on the right hand side are the two Ringel daughters, Elsa, with hat, and Emma. Photo circa 1912. *Photo courtesy Fort Walla Walla Museum #92.130.1*

Above: Delivery day at the John Smith Hardware Company on North Main Street in Waitsburg, circa 1910. Three steam engines with threshing machines hooked behind line the street. *Photo courtesy Henry V. "Bill" Zuger*

Left: Sawmill employees and a couple of boys pose for the photograph in Walla Walla, circa 1910. *Photo courtesy Fred L. Mitchell*

Far Left: Bergevin brothers harvesting crew near Walla Walla, circa 1910. Identified from left, exluding the man working on the tractor, are Leo Darling, Ray Berger, Merrill Anderson, Harlan Young, Clem Bergevin, Chas. Bergevin, Thomas Davis and Ray Judge. *Photo courtesy Claro E. Bergevin*

Walla Walla Valley Memories

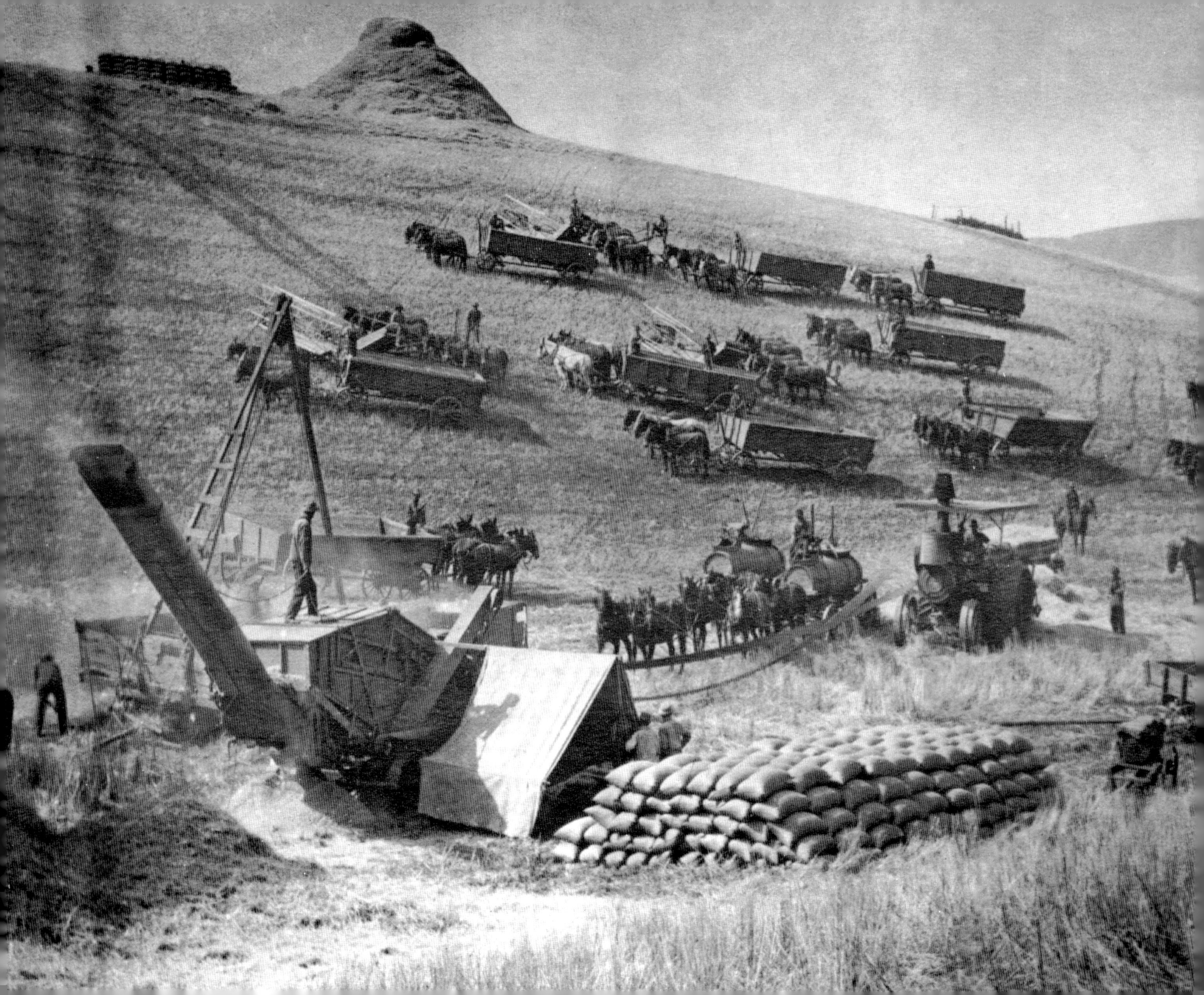

Above: Cook house of Zuger-Weller harvesting outfit, four miles west of Waitsburg, 1912. *Photo courtesy Henry V. "Bill" Zuger*

Left: Giuseppe Locati preparing to work in the fields, Walla Walla, 1913. *Photo courtesy Marilyn McCann*

Far left: Threshing outfit on the Marcus Zuger Jr. ranch, four miles west of Waitsburg, 1912. Included in this scene are 11 header boxes, three push headers, a steam engine and stationery harvester, and stacked wheat.

Photo courtesy Henry V. "Bill" Zuger

23

Above: Wheat harvesting outfit near Walla Walla in the early 1900s. The man at top center is identified as James Wallace Sherry. *Photo courtesy Debra Sherry*

Right: Apple picking in Walla Walla, circa 1915. *Photo courtesy Fred L. Mitchell*

Below: Thomas A. Adkins filling the water wagon for Beam's thrasher at Lookingbill Bridge on the Touchet River, 1915. *Photo courtesy Fred L. Mitchell*

Above: Saturno Farm off Myra Road, 1916. Pictured is Pasquale Saturno, third from left and his daughter, Josephine Saturno; three unidentified priests and a hired man, Joe Jermino. The man on the far left is unidentified. This group is standing in an onion field. At the time of this photo Pasquale had farmed for over 40 years. *Photo courtesy Douglas Saturno*

Above: John Merry on a hay derrick at a farm on Frog Hollow Road in the Touchet-Lowden area, circa 1917.
Photo courtesy John Merry

Left: Members of Walla Walla Gardeners' Association in front of their new North 11th Street shipping house, circa 1917.
Photo courtesy Don Locati

Walla Walla Valley Memories

Above: Ten teams of horses pulling spray wagons at the Baker Langdon orchard at the south end of 3rd Street, Walla Walla, circa 1923. Lead driver (on right) is Otto E. Suckow.
Photo courtesy Steven Suckow and Suckow family

Right: Horse drawn combine, combining cutting and threshing, and sack sewing in the 1920s. *Photo courtesy Fort Walla Walla Museum #76.32.3*

Below: Ernie Fehlberg and an unidentified man pose with Case Farm Equipment in 1925. From his experience as a field man for Case Farm Equipment Company, Ernie went on to develop the Fehlberg bulk tank in the late 1920s. *Photo courtesy Janice Eyestone*

Working the Land

Left: Robert Kibler with lamb on the Kibler Ranch, six miles east of Walla Walla, circa 1930.
Photo courtesy Robert Kibler family

Left: Harvesting crew standing in front of a cook wagon, circa 1928. This picture was taken by Donald McGregor of the McGregor Land and Livestock's stationary harvest operation on their Wood Gulch ranch southeast of Hooper. Back row: John Forrest, (straw boss, holding Johnny Forrest), Iva Forrest (cook), Velma Forrest (helper), Rhodes Archer, Henry Snyder (derrick man), "Tuffy" Davidson, unknown, unknown, unknown, unknown, unknown (header puncher with glasses on hat), Art Baldwin (sack buck), brother of Art Baldwin, Boyd Fagg (roustabout), unknown. Front row: unknown, Bill Baldwin (header puncher), Elmer Forrest (father of John), unknown, unknown, Mr. Long (engineer), Jack Archer, unknown, Joe Marmes (separator man – "Brains of the Crew"), unknown, Aaron "Buck" Fagg, Dallas A. Hooper (loader). Inside the cook house: Melvin Forrest, son of John, age 10.
Photo courtesy Fort Walla Walla Museum #85.48.3

Working the Land

Above: A scene at the Clem Bergevin Ranch, circa 1939. The men in the photo are identified from left as Oran Fore (on the horse), Clarence Bergevin, Ted Smith, Ben Moro and Clem Bergevin. *Photo courtesy Claro E. Bergevin*

Left: Harvesting scene at the Robison Ranch, Walla Walla, circa 1935. Mary Robison Lynch (in white shirt) is driving the wheat truck. This scene is particularly interesting because it shows the transition from horse power to motorized power. *Photo courtesy Margaret Lynch*

Above: Elmer Smith in the crows nest of combine and his dad Geo. W. Smith (with hands on hips), harvesting wheat on the Smith family farm in Clyde, 1930s.
Photo courtesy Geo. W. and Mabel Smith family, Shari Richmond and Frances Wright

Left: Henry Mohrland beet farming on La Buddies' place, near Prospect Point School, circa 1938. *Photo courtesy Nadine Christiano*

Walla Walla Valley Memories

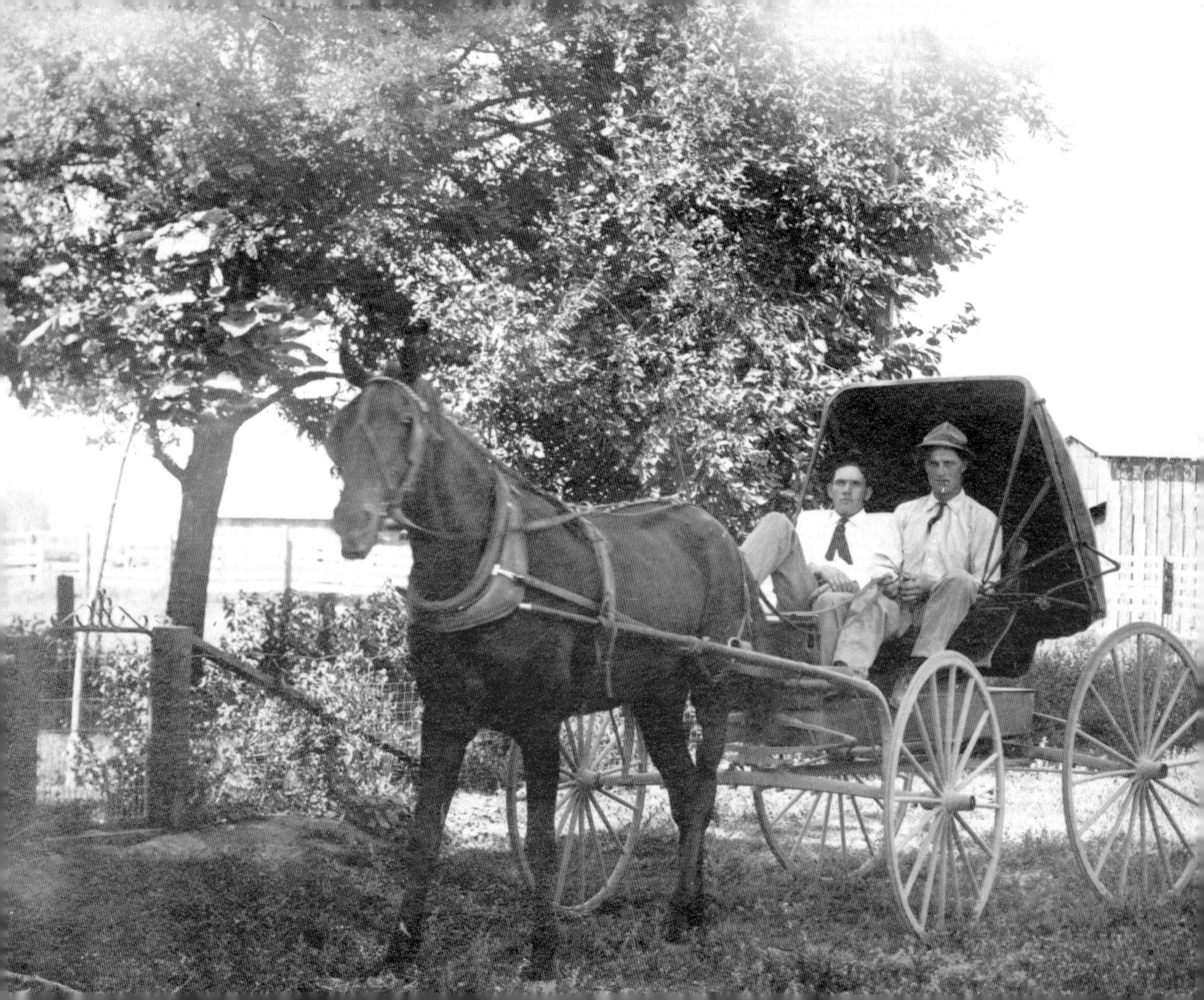

CHAPTER THREE
Transportation

The Walla Walla Valley would have remained largely untapped – and unpopulated – without improvements in transportation. In the early days, settlers and others arrived by horse, wagon, buggy and even by stagecoach. The introduction of trains made it easier to get here and to get local agricultural products to market.

America's love of automobiles was strong in this area and photographs from this era show the evolution of that mode of transportation. For those who didn't have their own automobile, getting around town was as simple as hopping on a streetcar, a bicycle, or for the more adventurous, a motorcycle.

Ferries, such as the one at Wallula, also played a role in keeping people and produce moving past the natural barriers of rivers and streams. Many automobile owners who miscalculated the depth of a stream found themselves looking for a helpful farmer with some old-fashioned transportation (horses or mules) to help pull their modern vehicle back to dry land.

Left: Sam Barnes and Audley Hansen aboard a horse drawn buggy in Touchet, circa 1900. *Photo courtesy Judy Largent Treman*

Right: Motor Car No. 1, "The InterUrban," the new Oregon-Washington Railroad and Navigation gas-powered motor car running between Dayton and Wallula via Walla Walla, circa 1910. *Photo courtesy Judy Largent Treman*

Above: The Abbot Stage line entering Walla Walla from Idaho, circa 1873.   *Photo courtesy Fred L. Mitchell*

Left: Woman in a horse-drawn wagon in front of a tin shop on 4th Street in Walla Walla, late 1800s.   *Photo courtesy Fred L. Mitchell*

Above: Public gathering at the Union Pacific Railroad station at West Main Street, Walla Walla.   *Photo courtesy Fort Walla Walla Museum #87.15.19*

Right: Engine 107 on the Oregon Railroad & Navigation Company (OR&N) line, at the west end of Main Street, circa 1895.   *Photo courtesy Fred L. Mitchell*

Left: Walla Walla and Columbia Railroad, formerly Baker Railroad in Wallula, 1895. The building shown is thought to be the O.R. & N. Hotel, which was removed in 1910. The town is behind the photographer.

Photo courtesy Fred L. Mitchell

Above: The Inter-Urban Railway Depot at the northeast corner of 6th and Main in Walla Walla. There is a railroad car beside the building that is now Snyder-Crecelius Company.   *Photo courtesy Fort Walla Walla Museum #95.42.31*

Left: Looking west on Alder Street from between Colville and 1st streets, Walla Walla, circa 1900. Delivery wagons are pulled by horses.

Photo courtesy Fort Walla Walla Museum #86.17.6

Right: The O. R. & N. train depot at the west end of Main Street in Walla Walla, 1908. The Genevay Hotel, at right, was located on Main Street.
Photo courtesy Fred L. Mitchell

Below right: Walla Walla Traction Co. trolley car No. 22, early 1900s.
Photo courtesy Douglas Saturno

Below: In 1901, Walla Walla extended electric trolley service to East Walla Walla. This trolley is located on Main Street in front of the courthouse. *Photo courtesy Fred L. Mitchell*

Transportation

Right: Dodge automobiles lined up in front of the Lennon Building, on the north side of Alder Street at Spokane Street, Walla Walla, 1920s.
Photo courtesy Douglas Saturno

Above: Street car in downtown Walla Walla, circa 1917. This view is from the corner of Main and 2nd streets, looking south.
Photo courtesy Fred L. Mitchell

Left: The J.M. Crawford family in the family car in front of their house at 1324 East Isaacs Avenue, Walla Walla, 1910. Behind the wheel is J.M. Crawford. Starting at left is Martha, his wife; children, Susan, Howard, and Harold. *Photo courtesy Margaret Lynch*

Below: D. W. McFaden in his horse-drawn buckboard on Abbot Road, 1904. *Photo courtesy Fred L. Mitchell*

Walla Walla Valley Memories

LONG DISTANCE TELEPHONE
TELEPHONE
Indian
Indian
Indian
Indian

Left: Group of Walla Walla telephone company employees on their Indian motorcycles, circa 1910. Second man from left is R.L. Britton; behind him is his daughter Louise Jaussaud Britton.

Photo courtesy Leontine Jaussaud Winn

Right: Streetcar in front of the First National Bank building at the corner of 2nd and Alder in Walla Walla, circa 1924.

Photo courtesy Francis Christiano

Above: Frank Jackson was a Harley Davidson dealer and he and some of his friends built this snowmobile. The photo was taken in front of his shop on East Alder Street, circa 1920. Next to Frank's shop was A.A. (Pops) Herring taxi service. Carmen Saturno is sitting in far back. *Photo courtesy Jack Jackson*

Left: Wallula gasoline-operated ferry takes passengers across the river, August 1918. *Photo courtesy Fort Walla Walla Museum #93.164.20*

39

Above: Harv Yenney in his car that got stuck in the stream, 1920s. *Photo courtesy Bert Yenney*

Right: A team of horses was needed to pull Harv Yenney's car out of the stream, 1920s. *Photo courtesy Bert Yenney*

Below: John H. Timmons, one of the last draymen in Walla Walla, with his dray, circa 1925. His dray is now in the Fort Walla Walla Museum. *Photo courtesy Susan Queen*

Right: Conductor Andrew Loucks stands in the doorway of a Union Pacific train in Walla Walla, circa 1924.

Photo courtesy Susan Queen

Left: Bicycling Jacksons at Pioneer Park, 1939. Pictured, from right are, Frank and Edna Jackson (owners of Jackson Sporting Goods), Ralph and Rachel Jackson, Harold and Gertie Jackson, Jack and Ethel (Jackson) Money, Dorothy Jackson Brashear, Ginger Jackson Kelly and Jack Jackson. Frank Jackson had the first bicycle shop in Walla Walla County. *Photo courtesy Ginger Kelly*

POSITIVELY NO
SMOKING ALLOWED
INTERNATIONAL
BROKERAGE CO.
APRIL
30
WEDNESDAY

CHAPTER FOUR

Commerce & Industry

Agriculture was the cornerstone of business in the Walla Walla Valley. But it quickly gave birth to a wide range of commerce to support it. Banks blossomed and flourished. Blacksmith shops, farm machinery companies, dry goods stores, canneries and flour mills sprouted as fast as the wheat and fruits and vegetables.

More businesses and services were then required to take care of the needs of those who were taking care of the farmers. Groceries, newspapers, hospitals, hotels, restaurants, bakeries, saloons, delivery services, laundries, furniture stores, insurance companies and many other types of businesses and services opened. This presented people with choices of jobs and careers and the opportunity to put down deep roots in the area.

The improvements in technology and transportation continued to nurture and improve the local business climate. As businesses thrived, the local economy began to become more and more diversified, making it less susceptible to downturns in any one area.

Left: Employees of Shaw & Baumeister Insurance, in Walla Walla, pose for the photographer in 1919. *Photo courtesy Fred L. Mitchell*

Right: Interior of G.W. Jones' grocery store, circa 1909. On the left is Bob Jones. The man on the right is George Washington Jones. *Photo courtesy Brenda*

Right: A large steel vat is created by H.M. Porter & Co. of Walla Walla, circa 1875. *Photo courtesy Douglas Saturno*

Far Right: Fourth of July cup and saucer contest at Delmonico's French Restaurant on Main Street in Walla Walla, circa 1895. The man in the center, Charles Lavan Parris, won the contest. The restaurant, also known as "The Happy Fat Man" and "The French Restaurant," was located across the street from the Dacres Hotel. *Photo courtesy Jeff Ray*

Above: Employees of the Walla Walla Statesman Newspaper, 1890.
Photo courtesy Fred L. Mitchell

Left: Stockwell's Paints & Oils on West Main, Walla Walla, 1890.
Photo courtesy Fort Walla Walla Museum #83.19.48B

Commerce & Industry

Above: Schwarz's Saloon at 120 West Main Street in Walla Walla, circa 1887.
Photo courtesy Francis Christiano

Right: Pioneer Grocery in the late 1800s. Maggie Draper is identified as the woman in the dark dress with Ella Draper at her side. Others are not identified.
Photo courtesy Matthew Seeliger

Above: Schwarz Building, owned by Adolph and Lulu (Stahl) Schwarz, at the southeast corner of 4th and Main streets, Walla Walla, late 1800s. The building was owned by the Schwarz family until 1991. *Photo courtesy Tracy Schwarz*

Left: Offices of the Walla Walla Statesman on 3rd and Alder. The building was built in 1890. *Photo courtesy Fred L. Mitchell*

Right: The General Blacksmithing shop operated by W.P. Powell.

Photo courtesy Fort Walla Walla Museum #86.9.3

Opposite page: Eureka Saloon on Main Street, between 4th & 5th streets, opposite Dacres Hotel, Walla Walla, circa 1900.

Photo courtesy Francis Christiano

Below right: Jacob Schubert "The Tailor" at his tailor shop in the Baker Boyer National Bank building at 2nd and Main streets, Walla Walla, 1897. He operated his business at this location for three to five years and then moved to a larger shop in Walla Walla. His tailoring business subsidized his farming operation.

Photo courtesy Patsy Poe

Below: Workers wait on the dock of the Walla Walla Produce Company as horse-drawn buggies deliver produce in crates, circa 1900. *Photo courtesy Fort Walla Walla Museum #02.1.73*

46   Commerce & Industry

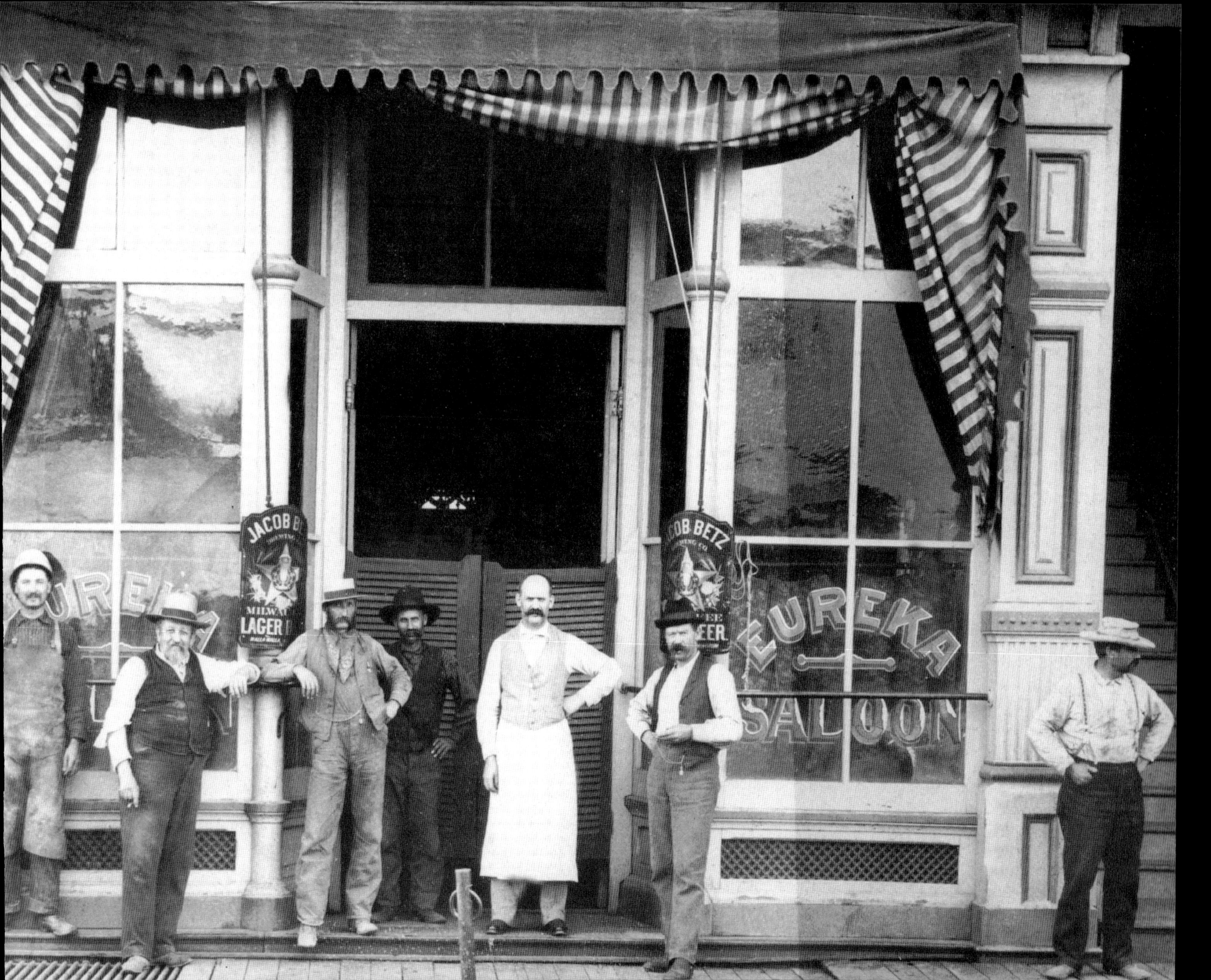
EUREKA
SALOON
JACOB BE
LAGER
COB BETZ

Above: Employees of Pacific Telephone and Telegraph Company pose atop a telephone pole, circa 1903.
Photo courtesy Leontine Jaussaud Winn

Above right: McFaden & Gorman farm machinery shop, Walla Walla, 1903. In the photo: Harry Weir, Chester Berryman, Dan Kyger, D.W. McFaden, J.E. Gorman.
Photo courtesy Fred L. Mitchell

Right: Wagon frames line the street in front of the Jones Building at the northeast corner of 2nd and Alder streets in 1901. D.W. McFaden stands right of door and D.M. Gorman is left of the door. This building burned in 1912. The Paine Building is at left.
Photo courtesy Fred L. Mitchell

Left: Drivers pose with horses and delivery wagons of the Walla Walla Steam Laundry, circa 1907. The business was owned by Eugene Tausick and employed more than 60 people.
Photo courtesy Fort Walla Walla Museum #88.16.1

Below left: A horse-drawn buggy delivers for The Jersey Dairy, circa 1905. Standing next to the horses is E.L. Waldron. The farm house in the picture is still standing in Lowden.
Photo courtesy Fort Walla Walla Museum #89.121.2

Below: Five men and a woman standing in front of the Bowman Bros. Plumbers building. There are three well pumps exhibited in front of their store window. On the right side of the building there are stairs going up and a sign saying "A. Garner -- Magnetic Healer."
Photo courtesy Fort Walla Walla Museum #95.41.3

Walla Walla Valley Memories

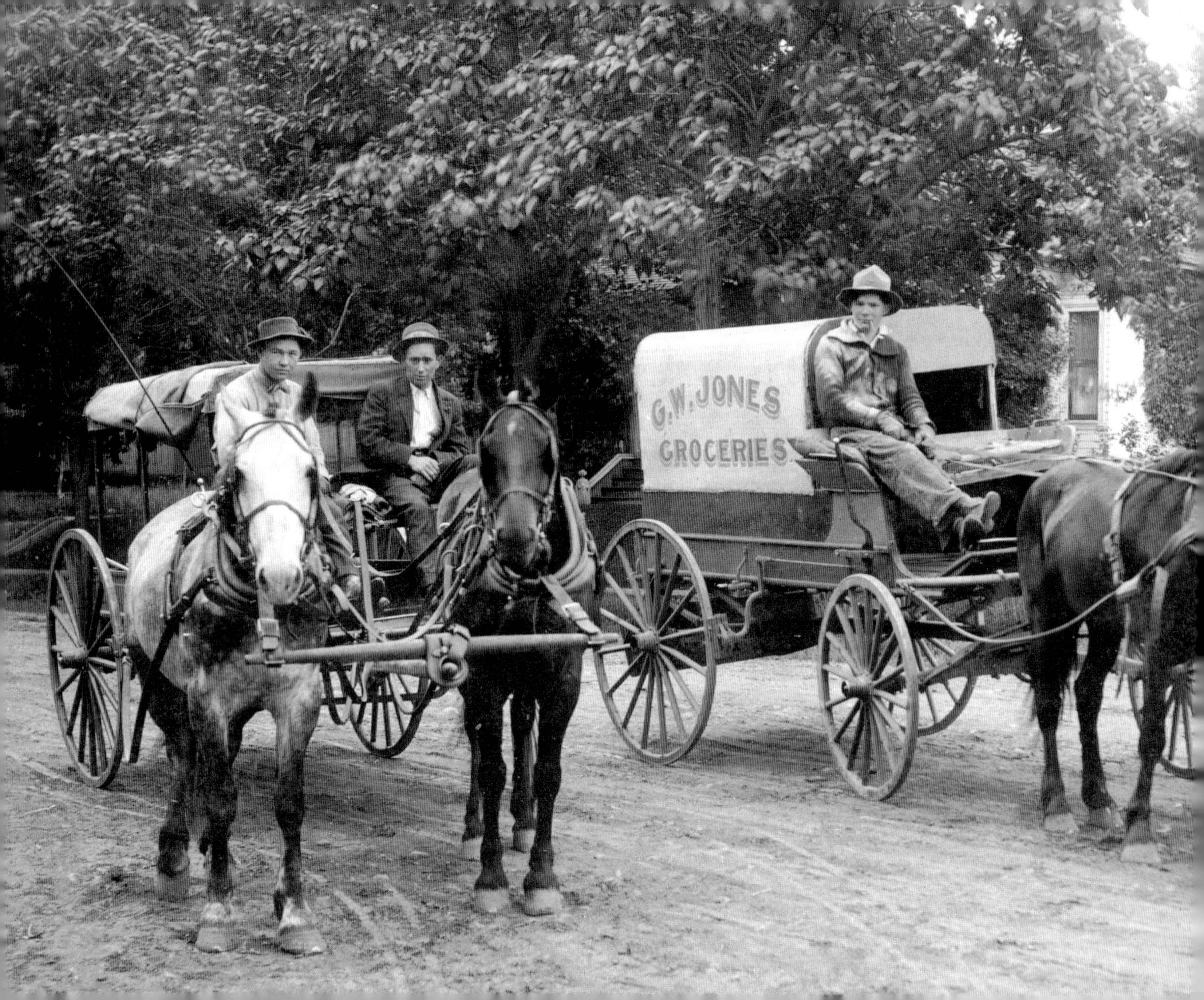
G.W. JONES
GROCERIES

Above: Electrical Workers Union 556 in Walla Walla, circa 1905.
Photo courtesy Leontine Jaussaud Winn

Left: Walla Walla Steam Laundry workers in the early 1900s.
Photo courtesy Matthew Seeliger

Far Left: Delivery wagons of G.W. Jones' grocery store in Walla Walla, circa 1900.
Photo courtesy Francis Christiano

Above: Walla Walla Pressery, circa 1905. *Photo courtesy Douglas Saturno*

Right: Cyrus H. Teal driving a horse-drawn wagon for Tausick-Kauffman, Walla Walla, 1910. He hauled 40 tons a day, earning $2 to $2.25 per day. *Photo courtesy Wanda G. Stimme*

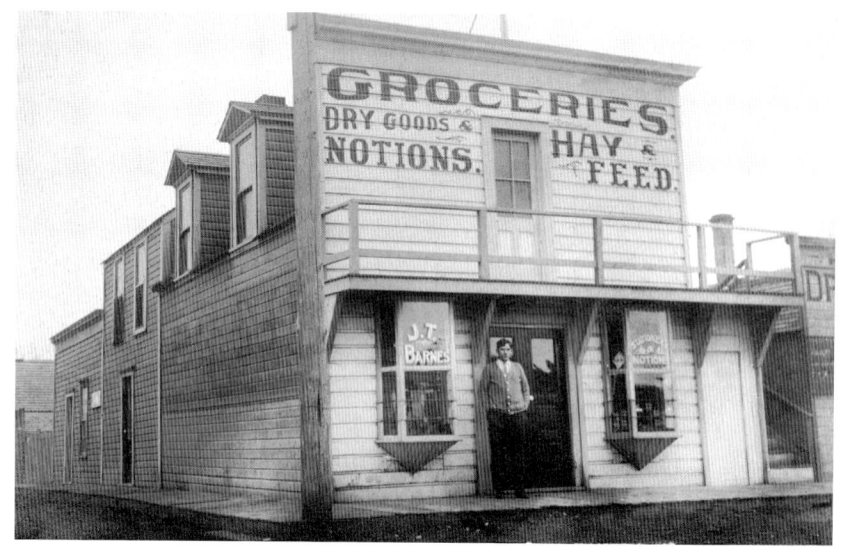

Above: J.T. Barnes in the doorway of his store on Main Street in Touchet, circa 1911. *Photo courtesy Judy Largent Treman*

Left: Employees of Bell Telephone Co., 100 block of East Alder, Walla Walla, circa 1906. Matilda Lonneker is pictured, third woman on the right. The location of this building later became a parking lot. *Photo courtesy Vicki Ueckert*

52

Commerce & Industry

Above: St. Mary's Hospital, at 5th and Poplar streets, was made of brick and was constructed after the old, wooden building burned down in 1915. *Photo courtesy Fort Walla Walla Museum #94.18.16*

Above: Dacres Hotel at the southwest corner of Main and 4th streets in Walla Walla, circa 1912. *Photo courtesy Fort Walla Walla Museum #01.13.1*

Left: The Grand Hotel on the northwest corner of 1st and Alder streets, Walla Walla, circa 1912.

Photo courtesy Fred L. Mitchell

Above and right: Pure White was a product of the Preston-Schaffer Milling Company. The promotional campaign became a Waitsburg community event. On this July day in 1912 (right photo) townspeople and mill workers gathered to witness the hoopla. Dale Preston, president of the milling company was on hand. He sat behind the driver's wheel of the first car. Driving the second car was Walter Woods, a local farmer. Next to him in the Franklin car and looking proper was Mr. Wheeler, editor of the Waitsburg Times newspaper. The engine in the background moved boxcars in and out of the mill siding as they were loaded with flour. The train operated between Pasco and Spokane.

Photos courtesy Fort Walla Walla Museum #UK.UK.967d (above) #UK.UK.967c(right)

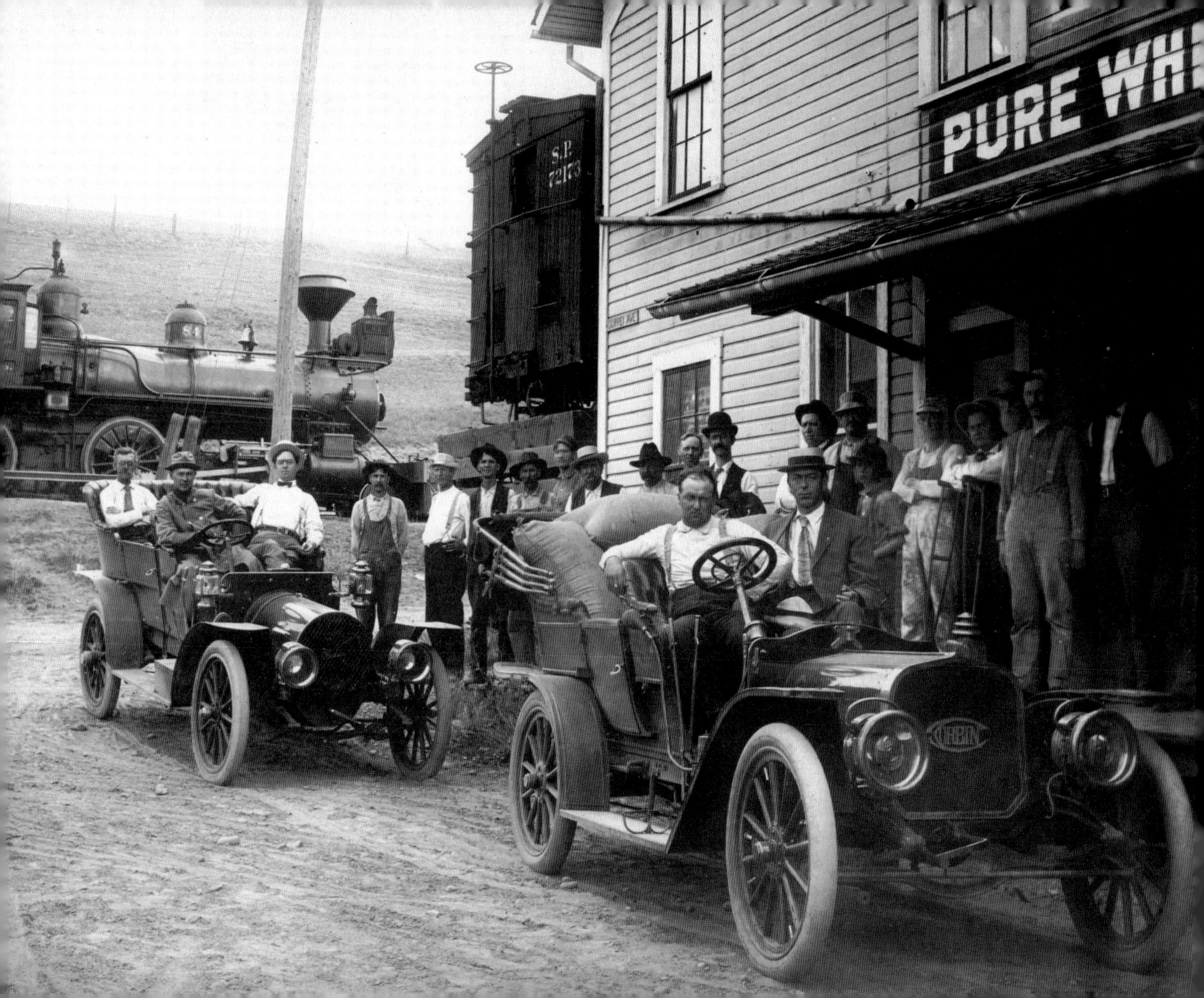
PURE WH
S.P.
72173
84

Above: Walla Walla Hospital on East Alder Street, circa 1916. *Photo courtesy Fort Walla Walla Museum #92.75.2*

Right: Baker Boyer Bank Building, built in 1910 at the corner of 2nd and Main streets, Walla Walla. Photo circa 1915. *Photo courtesy Fred L. Mitchell*

Below right: Confectionery Bakery in Walla Walla, circa 1915. *Photo courtesy Paul Webb*

Above: D.V. Wood Agency at 2nd and Poplar, Walla Walla, 1911. Pictured in the doorway are C.B. Lane, D.V. Wood, and Robert Wood.

Photo courtesy Douglas Saturno

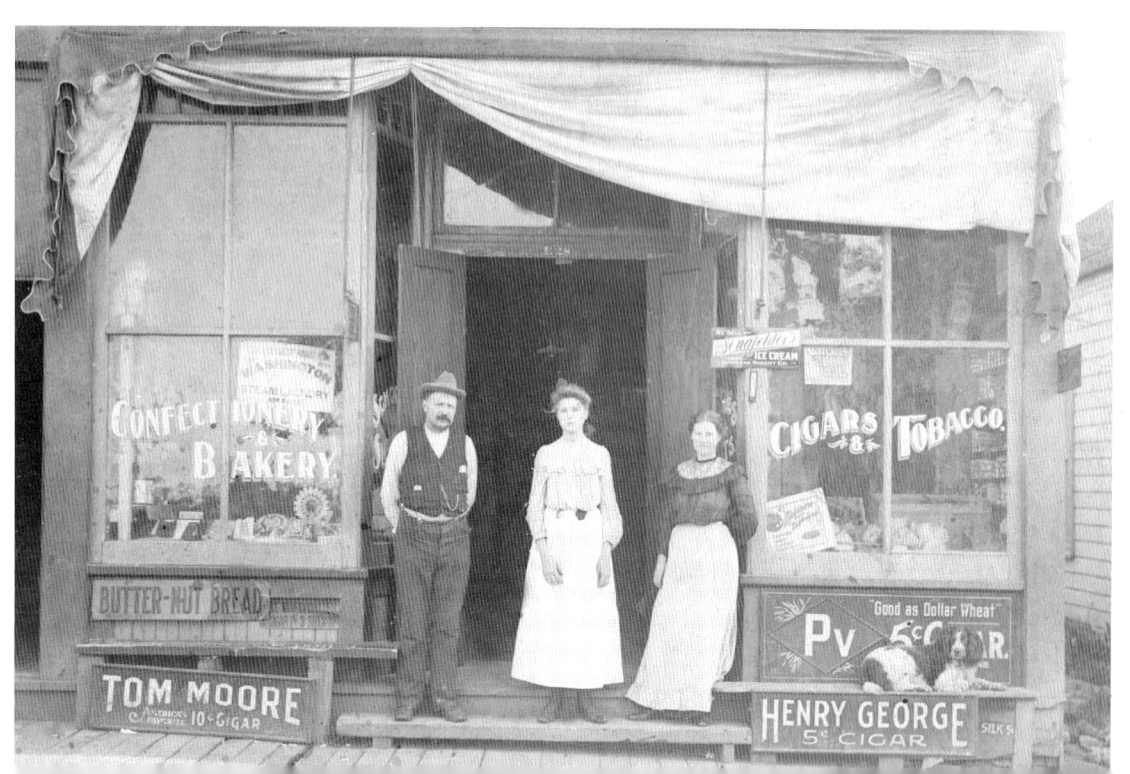

56

Right: East End Welding Works at 212 East Main Street, Walla Walla, 1920.

Photo courtesy Douglas Saturno

Above: Interior of Ed Priest meat market on Main Street in Pomeroy, 1916. Ed's son, Carl Priest, is pictured in a dark suit and hat. *Photo courtesy Donna Priest Gifford*

Left: Ed Priest meat market on Main Street in Pomeroy, 1916.

Photo courtesy Donna Priest Gifford

LOCAL UNION
Walla Walla
No. 377
U A
GAS FITTERS
STEAM FIT
PLUMBERS

Above: Interior of McBeth's Used Furniture store, Walla Walla, circa 1930. *Photo courtesy Douglas Saturno*

Left: The 1920 Plumber's Union, dressed in dusters and hats. *Photo courtesy Fort Walla Walla Museum #UK.UK.5396*

Left: Louie Fazzari inside the Pastime Café at 217 West Main Street, Walla Walla, 1928. This was a family-owned and operated restaurant for many years, just recently closing. Notice the liquor bar on the left side and candy and cigar on the right side. *Photo courtesy Dorothy Fazzari Criscola*

Below: Marcus Whitman Hotel, Second and Rose streets in Walla Walla, completed in 1928. *Photo courtesy Fred L. Mitchell*

Above: First National Bank building at 2nd and Alder streets, Walla Walla, circa 1931. *Photo courtesy Fred L. Mitchell*

Walla Walla Valley Memories

Above: The distinguished Liberty Theater, headlining Harold Lloyd in 1938, on Main Street, between Colville and 1st streets, Walla Walla. This theater was built in 1917 as the American Theater and was renamed Liberty Theater in 1926.
Photo courtesy Fort Walla Walla Museum #87.62.2

Below: A bartender behind the counter at the Liberty Pool Hall, circa 1931. The hall was owned by Angelo Locati and Leo Castamier at that time. *Photo courtesy Fort Walla Walla Museum #89.59.1*

Above: Allen's Ice Cream shop in the Triangle Building on Boyer Street, circa 1939. William A. "Pete" Allen was the owner, and the man in the photo was one of Allen's employees.
Photo courtesy Barbara Allen Griffin

Left: Four White Trucking Company dump trucks near Touchet, circa 1933. O.A. White's company worked on many regional projects including Bonneville Dam and Grand Coule Dam. Drivers identified as "Erna, Loren, Earl, and Johnie."
Photo courtesy Carol White Beulaurier

Commerce & Industry

Above: One of the most significant dates in Walla Walla's economic development is pictured here—the ground breaking ceremonies February 6, 1933, for the Walla Walla Canning Company plant. It marked the start of construction on the first actual food processing plant in the Blue Mountain district. Public officials and stockholders participating were, left to right: F. Lowden Jones, who became the general manager; Clyde Lester, stockholder; Dr. Arthur A. Campbell, member of the earliest Chamber of Commerce cannery committee; Eugene Tausick, stockholder; Dr. Frank Baker, director; John G. Kelley, president and director and generally credited with being the individual most responsible for the project; Oscar Drumheller, director; Mrs. Mamie L. Bennett, then secretary of the Chamber of Commerce and of the company; John M. Crawford of the Chamber of Commerce cannery committee; T.A. Williams, director; James T. Crawford, vice president and director; Lester Crites, assistant superintendent; Dominic Loiacono, a leading growers' representative of that period; B.M. Huntington, director; J.H. Cunningham, director; and holding the shovel, J.J. "Jake" Arnold, a distinguished cameraman of that time. *Photo courtesy Fort Walla Walla Museum #UK.UK.5592*

Left: Dave Mitchell, pictured right, canning peas in Walla Walla.
Photo courtesy Fred L. Mitchell

Walla Walla Valley Memories

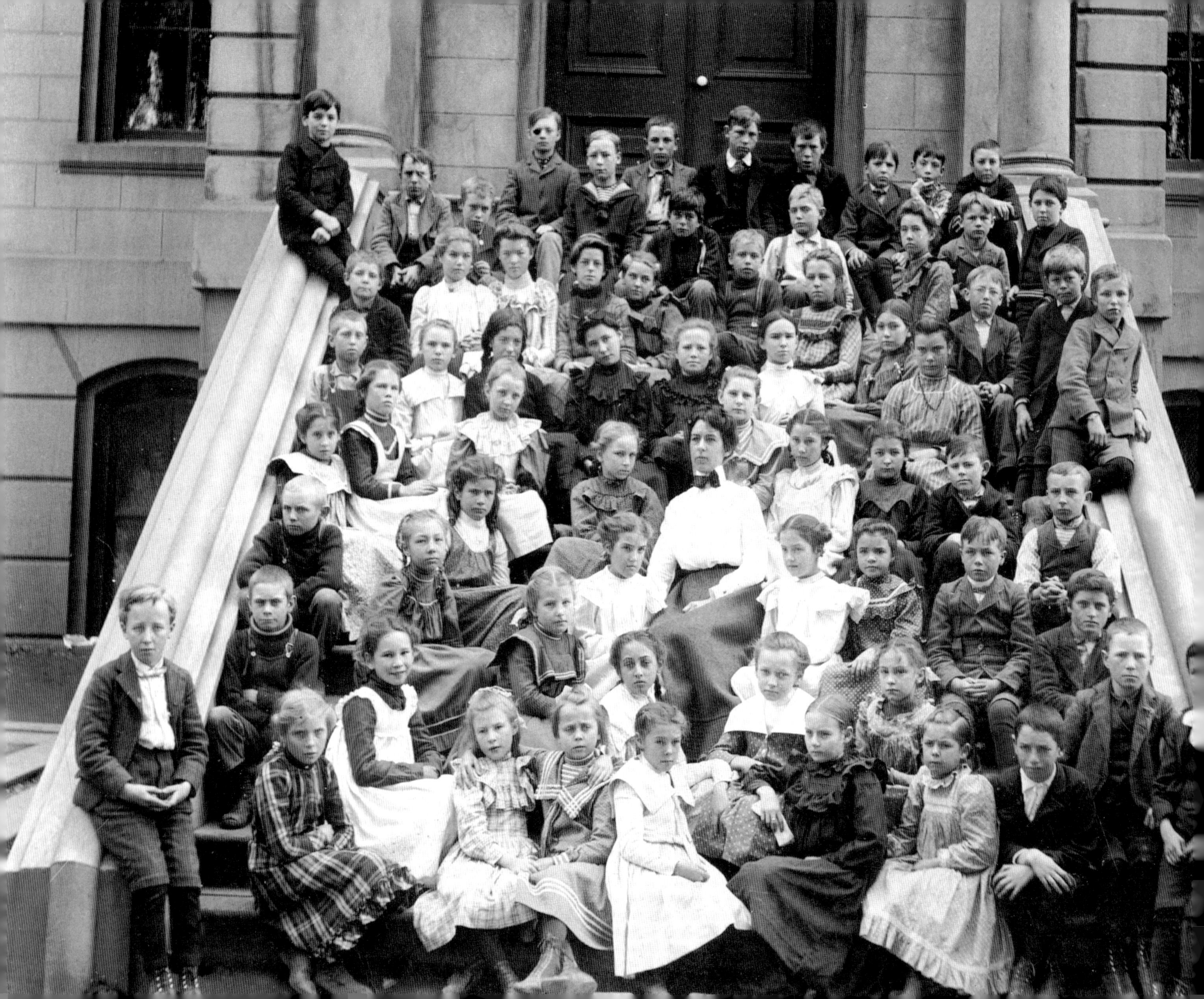

CHAPTER FIVE
Schools & Education

As more and more people discovered the wonders of the Walla Walla Valley and established the area as their home, families began to grow and the need for educational facilities became evident. Communities made this a high priority, and grade schools and high schools were quickly constructed. These structures were built to stand the test of time. Many of the schools from the early 20th century still remain in service. Some of them, such as Green Park and Sharpstein, have undergone renovations but have retained the style of their origins.

In most towns, the schools were a key part of the community, serving not only to educate the children but as a center for local activities. Communities took an undeniable pride in their schools and their youths. It was common for class photos to be taken in front of the school building.

Higher education was a unique possibility in the Valley with two colleges, Whitman College and Walla Walla College, tracing their origins back to the early days.

Sports have always played an important role in all levels of local schools. Football, baseball and basketball were very popular. Foreshadowing things to come, women participated in basketball at Whitman College prior to 1900.

Left: Fourth grade Baker School students pack on to these stairs outside the school to take a class photo in 1902. Their teacher was Bonnie Jean Painter. The school was located on Sumach Street between Palouse & Spokane streets.
Photo courtesy Fort Walla Walla Museum UK.UK.921

Right: Whitman College faculty on the porch of College Hall, Boyer Avenue, 1896. Top row, left to right: L.F. Anderson, Dr. Cooper, W.D. Lyman, Dr. Penrose, B.H. Brown, Dr. Bert Thomas; second row: W.A. Bratton, Helen A. Papoon, Mrs. Croue, Miss Loomis, and Otto A. Hauerbach. *Photo courtesy Fort Walla Walla Museum 83.19.73*

Right: Paine School, built in 1883, was four-stories tall and had a distinctive clocktower, as seen in this circa 1890 photo. The school was renamed Lincoln in 1902, condemned in 1926, reconstructed in 1927 and renamed Paine School.
Photo courtesy Fort Walla Walla Museum #93.137.19

Far Right: Manual training class at the Wallula School, circa 1880. Here, the boys are busy cobbling their own shoes. *Photo courtesy Fort Walla Walla Museum #UK.UK.5506*

Above: Children play in the yard of the Braden School and Cottage, 1880.
Photo courtesy Fort Walla Walla Museum #UK.UK.5479

Left: Students at the first Waitsburg Academy, late 1800s.
Photo courtesy Fort Walla Walla Museum #89.153.1

Schools & Education

Above: St. Paul's School, class of 1899. Pictured, back row: Maddie, Eva Switzler, Edith Moffet, Tat Ryger, Anne Taylor, Verna Duelley, Laura Copeland, Harriett (Lalle) Ankney, Ada, May Miller. Second row: Charity Ankney, Edna Stone, Margaret Boyer, Hallie Cropp, Helen Brents, Camille Goldman, Isabelle Bayer, Blanche Young, Myrtle Estes, Louise Chamberling, Hazel Jaycox, Nadine Welch. Third row: Katherine, Pearl Cavelier, Bessie, Lena Evans, Tess Snyder, Ednid Smutten, Bernice. Front row: Elron, Wallace, Howard Baker, Dick Burford, Smutton, Mark Darron, and Arthur Bayer. *Photo courtesy Fort Walla Walla Museum #83.19.48D*

Above left: Reynolds Hall, a three story brick building on the Whitman College Campus. *Photo courtesy Fort Walla Walla Museum #87.15.16*

Left: The domestic science class at the College Place School, circa 1890. *Photo courtesy Fort Walla Walla Museum #UK.UK.5501*

65

Above: St. Patrick School students, Walla Walla, circa 1900.
Photo courtesy Charles Joe Tompkins

Right: The first girl's basketball team at Whitman College, 1899. Team members included: Eliza Ramsey, Annie Barrett, Melissa Thomas, Bethene Crayne, Orva Greene, Arminda L. Fix, Leonore Bailry, Irma Rupp, Mabel Kelso, and Alice Gentry. The team started at least two years earlier.
Photo courtesy Fort Walla Walla Museum #UK.UK.930

Above: Third and fourth grade students inside their classroom at Sharpstein School. Pictured in row one: Houston Marshall, Myrtle Biersner, Rita Sturm, Howard Statsman, Miss Elva Griffith (teacher). Second row: Chesel Young, Ruth Beck, Dessie Tighe, Earl Richmond, Marge Palrick, Alma Burnett, Verla Hussey, Edwin Carters. Third row: Roy Noland, Hans (Pete) Hansen, Stanley Brock, Dorey Marsh, Evelyn Lamnero, Gaylord Thompson, Edna May. Fourth row: Franklin Beatty, Bernie Campbell, Othel Corkrum, and Dorothy Powers. *Photo courtesy Fort Walla Walla Museum #82.27.4*

Right: Moore School students pose with the American flag, 1900.
Photo courtesy Fort Walla Walla Museum #94.86.7

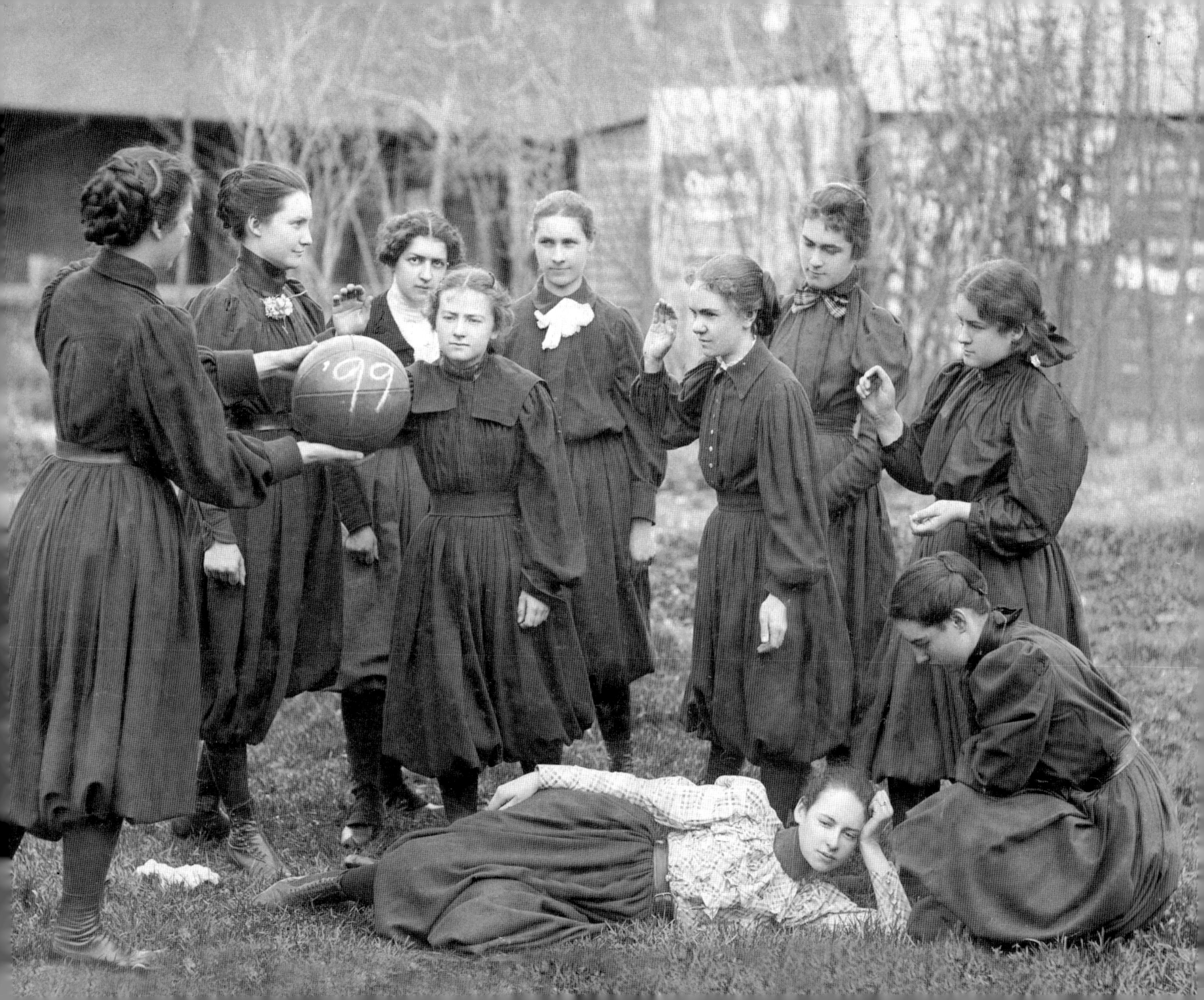
'99

Left: Classroom and students from St. Vincent Academy pose for the photographer, Walla Walla, circa 1900. *Photo courtesy Barbara Allen Griffin*

Above: St. Vincent Academy students, Walla Walla, 1900. *Photo courtesy Barbara Allen Griffin*

Right: Walla Walla High School football team of 1899. Standing in the back from left, Bert Delaney (holding the ball), captain and end; Albert Stewart, center; Clifford Minnick, tackle; and Lacey Galbraith, manager. Seated immediately in front of those standing are George Gray, halfback; Ed Emigh, quarterback; George Thompson, guard; Fred Bowman, tackle; and Archie Gilham (directly in front of Gilbraith), end. Front row, from left, Fred Brunton, guard; W.G. "Bill" Coleman (immediately behind Brunton), fullback; Ray Sutherland, reserve; Charles Hendrick, end; and Rudolph Rupp, halfback. *Photo courtesy Fort Walla Walla Museum #UK.UK.7491*

Above: Walla Walla High School Football Team of 1905. At right front, kneeling, is Grova C. Cookerly, who later became Walla Walla City Engineer. *Photo courtesy Claire Coryell Siegel*

Right: Walla Walla High School graduating class of 1906. *Photo courtesy Claire Coryell Siegel*

Above: Children who attended the Poplar Grove School in 1905. The Poplar Grove School was the first school in the area. Students came from Dry Creek on the Middle Waitsburg Road, Waggoner Road, and Lower Waitsburg Road. The school house was built on the Miller place in a poplar grove of trees. It was later moved to the corner of Martin Road and renamed Bourgeois School. *Photo courtesy Fort Walla Walla Museum #92.138.1*

Left: Walla Walla College at College Place, circa 1904.
Photo courtesy Fort Walla Walla Museum #06.24.2

Walla Walla Valley Memories

Schools & Education

Above: Green Park School, built in 1906, located on the northeast corner of Isaacs Avenue and Clinton Street, Walla Walla, 1908.
Photo courtesy Fred L. Mitchell

Left: Touchet High School students in front of their school, early 1900s.
Photo courtesy Judy Largent Treman

Far Left: Washington School football team, Walla Walla, 1908. Professor Stafford is also pictured. *Photo courtesy Fort Walla Walla Museum UK.UK.1882*

Walla Walla Valley Memories

71

Right: Berney School, on Pleasant Street at School Avenue, Walla Walla, circa 1910. *Photo courtesy Fred L. Mitchell*

Below: Prescott School, circa 1914. This school was built in 1913 at a cost of $35,000. *Photo courtesy Fort Walla Walla Museum #UK.UK.5539B*

Above: Washington School group, circa 1907. *Photo courtesy Susan Queen*

Left: A group of boys seated at desks in a classroom at La Salle School, circa 1910. The teacher is standing at the back of the room. *Photo courtesy Fort Walla Walla Museum #03.31.14*

Schools & Education

Above: A team of horses were hitched to the Lewis Peak School house to move the school to its new location, circa 1912. *Photo courtesy Fort Walla Walla Museum #UK.UK.5477*

Left: Green Park School students, Walla Walla, 1913.
Photo courtesy Janet Headley

Above: Sharpstein graduating class, Walla Walla, circa 1912.
Photo courtesy Karin Western

Right: Green Park Baseball Team from Walla Walla, circa 1913, with the Stall & Dean Championship cup. The only one identified is Harry Gilbert Jr. in the front row, far right. *Photo courtesy Janet Headley*

Right: First grade class photo, Berney School, 1914. Pictured left to right, top row: Earl Richmond, Judd Kimball, Houston Marshall, Hans Hansen, Bud LeRoux, Thomas Haggerty, Lannes Loiseau, Elbert Hunt, D.V. Jones, Dorsey Marsh, Chesel Young; second row: Loiseau, Sturn, Evelyn Lammers, Eva Jensen, Evan Berney, Evelyn Trimble; bottom row: Lorraine Schneller, Leta Berry, Blanche Biersner, Ruth Beck, and Rose Curcio. The teacher was Miss Hines. *Photo courtesy Fort Walla Walla Museum #82.27.6*

Above: Sharpstein School, built in 1908, circa 1913. *Photo courtesy Virgil Reynolds*

Left: The La Salle baseball team with the Stall & Dean Championship cup, 1914. In the back row, fourth from left, is Bill Beaver; sixth from left, Reinard Beaver; far right, Bill Bowe. *Photo courtesy Fort Walla Walla Museum #03.31.15*

Right: Walla Walla High School band members, 1913. Horace Berg was the band leader. *Photo courtesy Fred L. Mitchell*

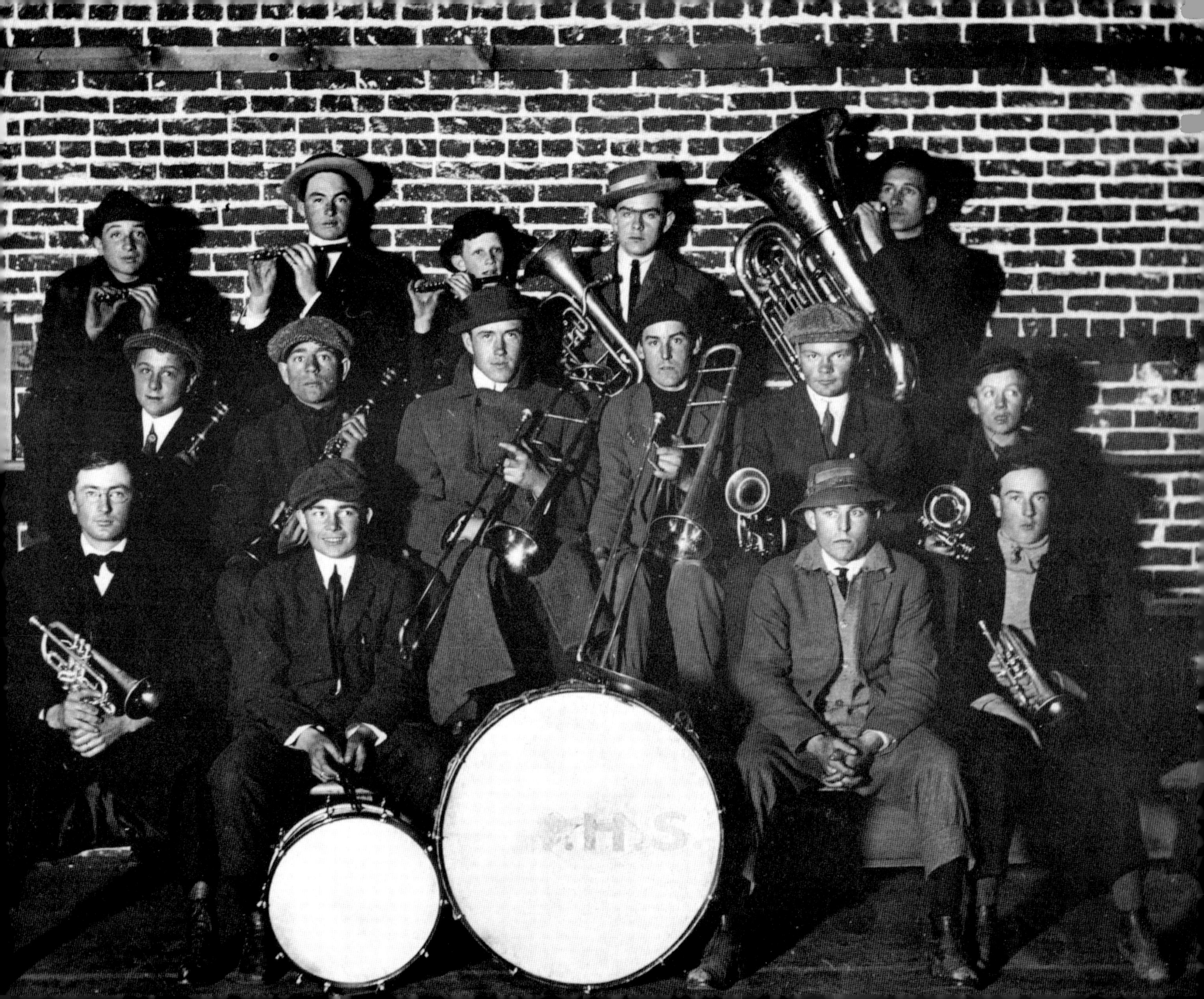

Right: School children play in the yard of Paul School House, 1916. *Photo courtesy Fort Walla Walla Museum #92.19.1*

Above: Whitman Memorial Building at Whitman College, Walla Walla, 1914. *Photo courtesy Fred L. Mitchell*

Left: Pettyjohn School in Prescott, 1915. Pictured, back row, from left: Melvin Ham, Sam Grant, Lawerence Pettyjohn, Elda Grant, Ivory Ray, Lee Boyd, Myrtle Ray, Arita Sharp. Front row: Wanda Ray, Dollie Ham, Goldie Ray, Albert Ham, and Charlotte Utter. The teacher was Earl Messenger. *Photo courtesy Fort Walla Walla Museum #RP.92.142.2*

Schools & Education

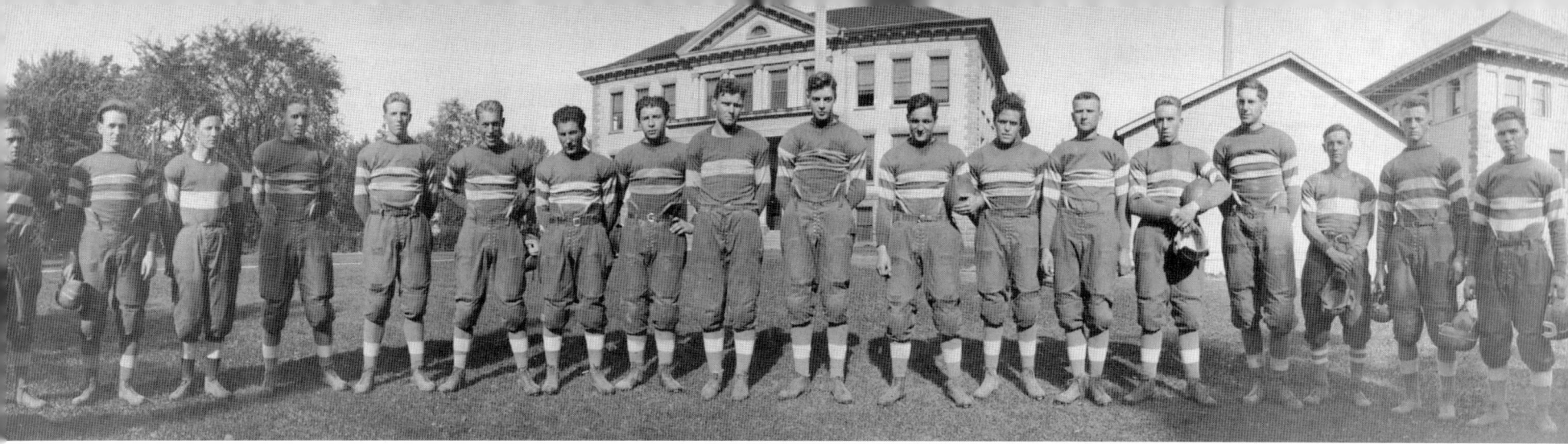

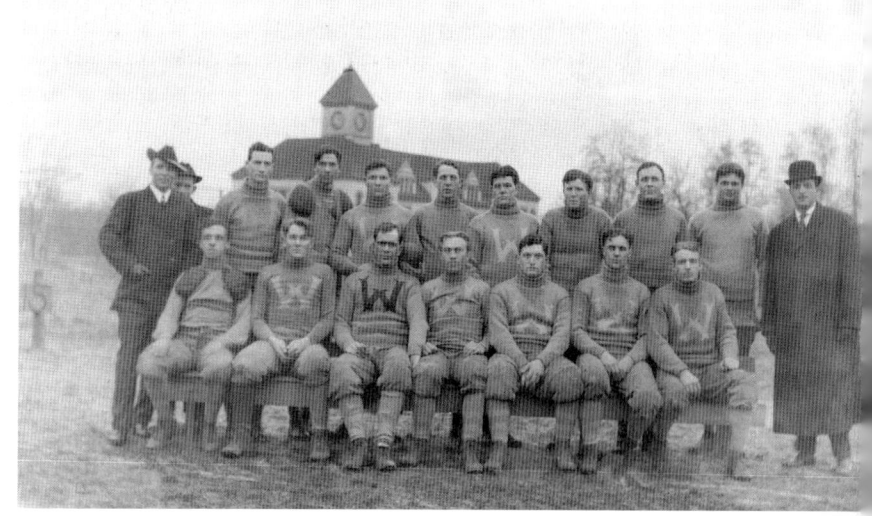

Above: Whitman College football team, Walla Walla, early 1900s. *Photo courtesy Fred L. Mitchell*

Left: Walla Walla High School football team, 1917. This team was the Western Champions with a record of 7-0. They outscored their opponents 363 to 30 including a 41-0 win over Pendleton and an impressive 119-0 win over Yakima. *Photo courtesy Fred L. Mitchell*

Top: Walla Walla High School football team, 1915. The high school can be seen in the background. *Photo courtesy Fred L. Mitchell*

BANNER CLASS

Above: Students and their teacher standing on the steps at Lincoln School, 1919.
Photo courtesy Fort Walla Walla Museum #93.155.175

Left: Students outside Baker School, north side of Sumach street, between Palouse and Spokane streets, Walla Walla, in the 1920s. *Photo courtesy Fort Walla Walla Museum #03.25.187*

Far Left: The Baptist Church in Walla Walla had a class once a week to teach Chinese students reading and other skills. The class was taught by Ruby Grosse, who taught in Walla Walla for 44 years, retiring in 1959. This photo includes students from a class in 1924. *Photo courtesy Fort Walla Walla Museum #87.76.1*

Left: Jefferson School basketball team that won the city championship in 1929.
Photo courtesy Claudia Bastron Huntley

Far Left: The St. Mary Nursing School, class of 1929.
Photo courtesy Fort Walla Walla Museum #03.21.2

Above: Dixie Elementary School first and second grade students, Dixie, 1929. Robert Kibler is identified as the third from the right, back row. Miss Henchaw was the teacher.
Photo courtesy Robert Kibler family

Right: Ferndale School children, 1920. The school was on the old highway between Walla Walla and Milton-Freewater.
Photo courtesy Shirley Dickerson

Schools & Education

Left: Washington School students on the lawn in front of the school, circa 1935.

Photo courtesy Nadine Christiano

Above: Student body of St. Vincent Academy, Walla Walla, circa 1935.

Photo courtesy Kathy Stritzel

Right: Walla Walla High School State Champion basketball team, 1934. The manager is McDaniels and the coach is Dimick. The others are listed by their number. Fouts (4), Onstot (5), Cunnington (6), Miller (7), Lockhart (8), LeRoy Bastron (9), Capt. Porter (11), Laman (13). *Photo courtesy Claudia Bastron Huntley*

Right: Green Park School 8th graders, 1937. Pictured are: Eleanor Scheece (teacher), Jean Jacobs, Edith Pope, Clayton Robberson, Pauline Fletcher, June Schmeltzer, Mildred Cannon, Elizabeth Vahe, Ella Mae Appling, Virginia Pratt, Lenore Russell, Lois Moulton, Luetta Anderson, Betty Anderson, Doris McCauley, Jerry LaRue, Charles Montgomery, Teddy Rich, Robert Hartley, John Darch, Jay Kerr, Lester Howard, Lila Stimmel, Bobby Teal, Geraldine Vail, Loche Van Otta, Helen Webb, Araid Johnson, Orval Stimmel, Patricia Stoover, Donald Caston, Wanda Hawkins, Walter Reely, Doris Bradford, Ralph Crampton, Mildred Bradford, Mildred Hector, Nadine Colley, Richard Robinson, Jack Kenney, Barbara Kain, Helen Fritsche, Helen Stine, Isabell Thomas, Alberta L. Brown, Edith L. Russel, Flora J. Becker, Grace Jensen, Eloise Thomas, Laura P. Olson, Thelma M. Nayes, and Betty Sue Martin. *Photo courtesy Fort Walla Walla Museum #05.32.6*

Left: College Place School children, 1939. Pictured, back row: Sherman Lehman, Frank Magnaghi, Stanley Beck, Bobby Russel, Bobby Wasser, Wilburt Biagi. Third row: Norman Miller, John Todorovich, Jake Wacker, Lawrance Locati, Robert Angell, Johnny Manuel, Elmer Sama, Junior Dunn. Second row: Roberta Bishop, Aileen Watkins, Audrey Angell, Christina Miller, Joybelle Dotson, Frances Smith, Emily Jean Curcio. First row: Marian Buerstatte, Arlene Vietz, Estelle Maxwell, Eleanor Grassi, Janell Haines, Geraldine Manuel, Barbara Swegle, Miriam Armstrong, Lila Ogden.
Photo courtesy Fred L. Mitchell

Right: School bus and staff of College Place School, 1936. J. Morton, janitor; L.A. Bender, principal; Gladys Harmon, 7th and 8th-grade; Glen Hastings, bus driver; Thora Linrud, 7th and 8th-grade; Esther Chapman, 1st-grade; Carrie Brown, 4th-grade; Louise Pettijohn, Emma Buehlen, 5th-grade; Doris Fogarty, 6th-grade; Ruth Auker, 2nd-grade; Mildred Dodd, 3rd-grade; Lucille Crawford, music. *Photo courtesy Fred L. Mitchell*

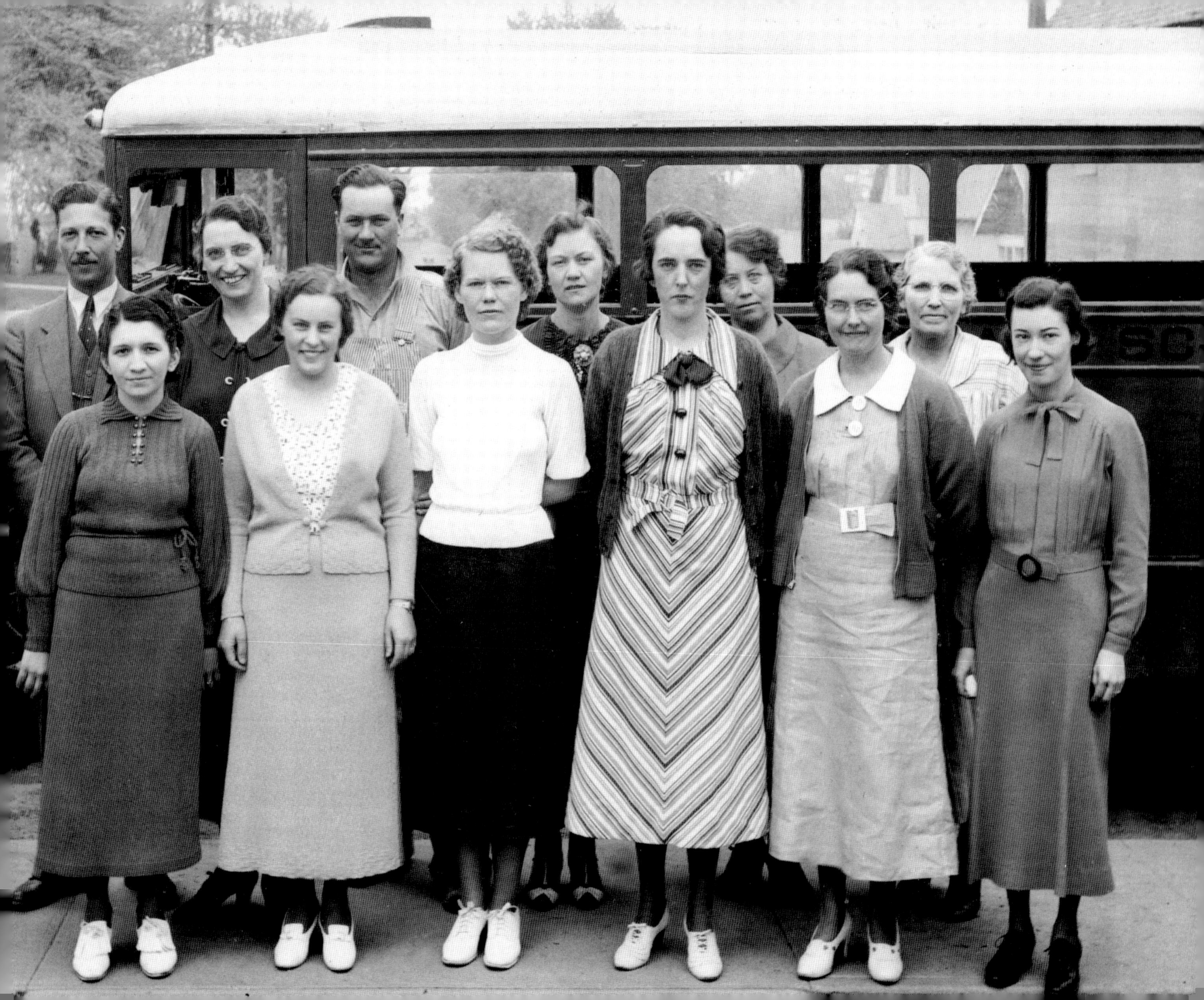

CHEAP
COUNTER STORE
.TOYS.
FURNITURE
STOVES AND TINWARE
BARGAIN STORE
TOYS,
NOTIONS
AND

CHAPTER SIX
Tradition of Public Service

There has been a military presence in the Walla Walla Valley almost from the time the first settlers arrived. Fort Walla Walla established a tradition of military service that continues today. Many buildings from the old fort remain at the grounds of the local veterans' hospital.

From the early days until 1939, troops and members of the National Guard from Walla Walla have done their duty in numerous military conflicts ranging from the Indian Wars, Spanish-American War, Philippine–American War, Mexican Punitive Expedition, and World War I.

In addition to the military, personnel from the state penitentiary, police and fire departments have endeavored to keep local citizens safe. While their duties are essentially the same now as they were then, changes in equipment, staffing levels and philosophies have been noted over the years.

Public offices for city and county governments were established to serve the public's needs. The courthouses in Walla Walla County and Columbia County have benefited from some recent renovations but remain familiar landmarks.

Left: Company I, 1st Battalion, Spanish-American War, on the main street in Walla Walla, circa 1898. Many of the soldiers were from Walla Walla.
Photo courtesy Fort Walla Walla Museum #UK.295.1

Right: Funeral for Assistant Fire Chief Robert J. Wolf, 1912. The photo was taken alongside the courthouse. Pictured, from left, Jake Kauffman, Dr. Yancy Blalock, Tom Casey, John Casey, Tom Pickard, Mike Davis, Chief Bill Metz. Seated are Tom Doroty and Hennesy. Wolf died January 26, 1912, in the Jones Building fire, 2nd and Alder streets, Walla Walla. *Photo courtesy Fred L. Mitchell*

Above: W.H. Bender, Walla Walla fireman, 1870.
Photo courtesy Fred L. Mitchell

Above right: Walla Walla hose team, late 1890s.
Photo courtesy Fred L. Mitchell

Right: Warden Frank Paine and the first guards at the Washington State Penitentiary, 1887. *Photo courtesy Fort Walla Walla Museum #UK.191.4*

Far Right: Guard tower at the State Penitentiary, Walla Walla, late 1800s.
Photo courtesy Fred L. Mitchell

Tradition of Public Service

Right: Indian Scouts from Fort Walla Walla, circa 1885.
Photo courtesy Fred L. Mitchell

Far Right: Soldiers stand at attention in front of the army barracks at Fort Walla Walla, circa 1898.
Photo courtesy Fort Walla Walla Museum #86.17.1

Above: Walla Walla Fire Department, circa 1895.
Photo courtesy Fort Walla Walla Museum #05.34.20

Left: The County Auditor's office in Walla Walla, circa 1895.
Photo courtesy Fort Walla Walla Museum #84.22.1

Walla Walla Valley Memories

Left: Corporal Charles W. McKean and fellow soldier of Company I, First Washington Volunteers (from Walla Walla), off to fight in the Spanish-American War, 1898. *Photo courtesy Fred L. Mitchell*

Far Left: The 4th Cavalry leaving Walla Walla for the Philippines in 1898. *Photo courtesy Fred L. Mitchell*

Above: The 4th Cavalry on board their train to leave Walla Walla for deployment to the Philipines in 1898. *Photo courtesy Fred L. Mitchell*

Right: Crowd gathers to send off the 4th Cavalry leaving Walla Walla for the Philippines in 1898. *Photo courtesy Fred L. Mitchell*

Left: James McAuliff, elected as mayor of Walla Walla for 11 terms. He came to Walla Walla in 1859. Photo circa 1898.
Photo courtesy Fred L. Mitchell

Below: Members of the Walla Walla Fire Department pose with their horse-drawn apparatus in front of the fire house, circa 1904.
Photo courtesy Fort Walla Walla Museum #UK.295.4

Above: City employees, police, fire, and city council, 1903. *Photo courtesy Fred L. Mitchell*

Right: First Lieutenant, Tom Hart, 2nd Regiment, National Guard of Washington, late 1800s. *Photo courtesy Fred L. Mitchell*

Walla Walla Valley Memories

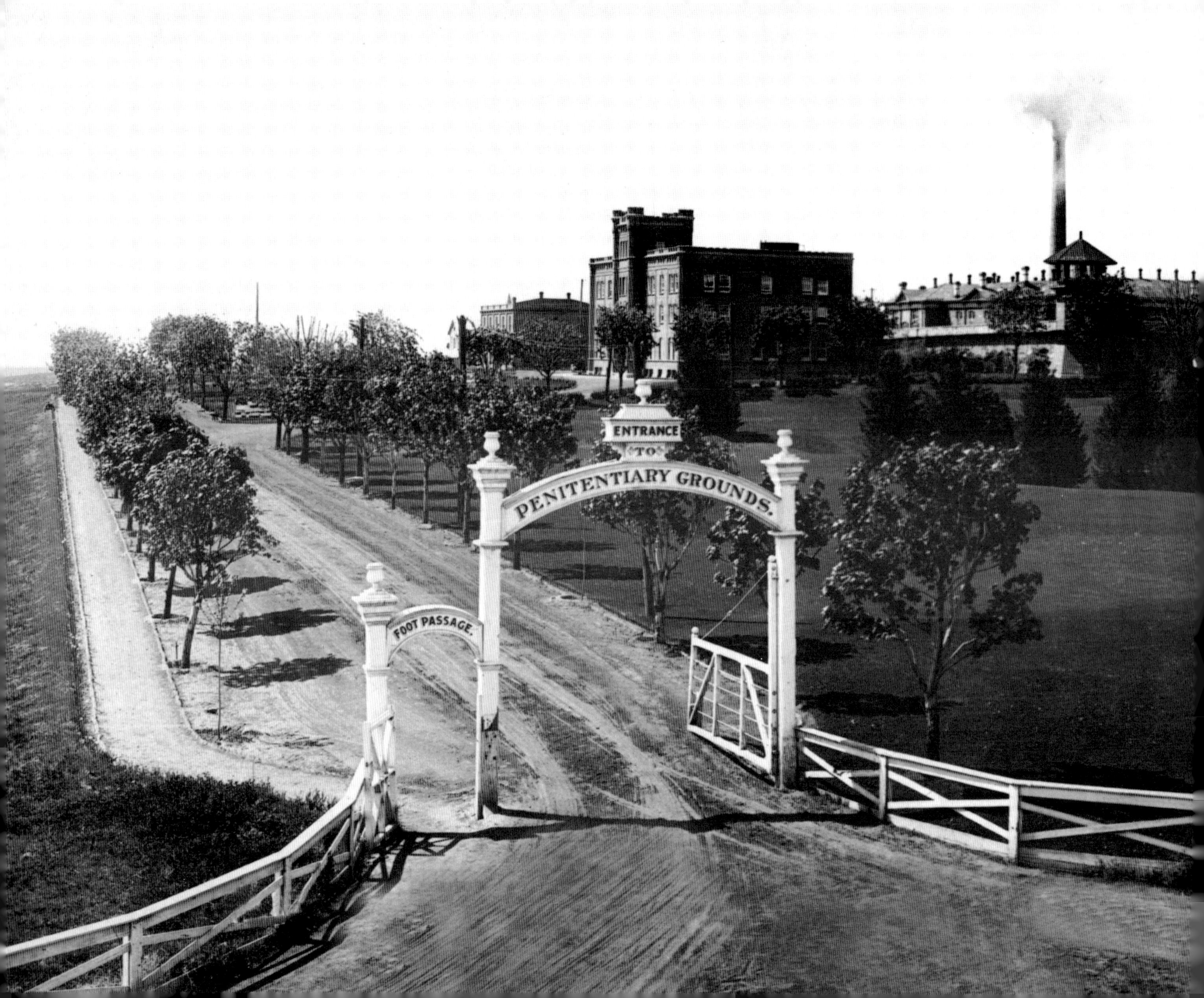
ENTRANCE
TO
PENITENTIARY GROUNDS.
FOOT PASSAGE.

Above: Walla Walla Fire Department Fire Station No. 2 at Park and Alder streets, shortly after its construction in 1904. The tower was used to dry hoses. *Photo courtesy Fort Walla Walla Museum #06.24.2*

Left: Entrance to the Washington State Penetentiary in Walla Walla, circa 1905. *Photo courtesy Virgil Reynolds*

Right: Walla Walla water sprinkling wagons line up for the photograph in this 1908 photo. Notice St. Patrick's Church in the background.
Photo courtesy Douglas Saturno

Below: Members of the Walla Walla Fire Department pose with the city's early mechanized fire truck, circa 1911. *Photo courtesy Francis Christiano*

Left: A front view of Walla Walla's early mechanized fire truck, circa 1911. The man behind the wheel is identified as Carl Gregory. The man on the left (hanging outside the car) is George Guthridge.
Photo courtesy Francis Christiano

Tradition of Public Service

Above: Bird's eye view of Fort Walla Walla, circa 1917. The area just north of the old fort buildings was used as an aviation field.
Photo courtesy Fort Walla Walla Museum #UK.UK.1327

Above left: Fire chief and fire fighters in front of the Fire Station No. 1 on Rose Street, Walla Walla, circa 1915.
Photo courtesy Douglas Saturno

Left: Company K, National Guard, leaves Walla Walla for the Mexican border in 1916 from the Northern Pacific Depot, at 2nd and Pine streets, as a large crowd wishes them farewell. *Photo courtesy Fort Walla Walla Museum #81.4.4*

95

Above: Battery A, Washington Field Artillery (146th Artillery), Fort Walla Walla. Recruiting began July 19 and the unit left Walla Walla on October 9, 1917.

Photo courtesy Fort Walla Walla Museum #01.28.1

Right: Members of the Walla Walla Police Department pose on the steps of City Hall, 3rd Street, circa 1920.

Photo courtesy Douglas Saturno

Tradition of Public Service

Left: Buildings and grounds of the United States Veterans' Administration Hospital located in Walla Walla on the grounds of old Fort Walla Walla. It was a fort from 1858 until 1910, and was reopened briefly during World War I. *Photo courtesy Fort Walla Walla Museum #96.2.39*

Walla Walla Valley Memories

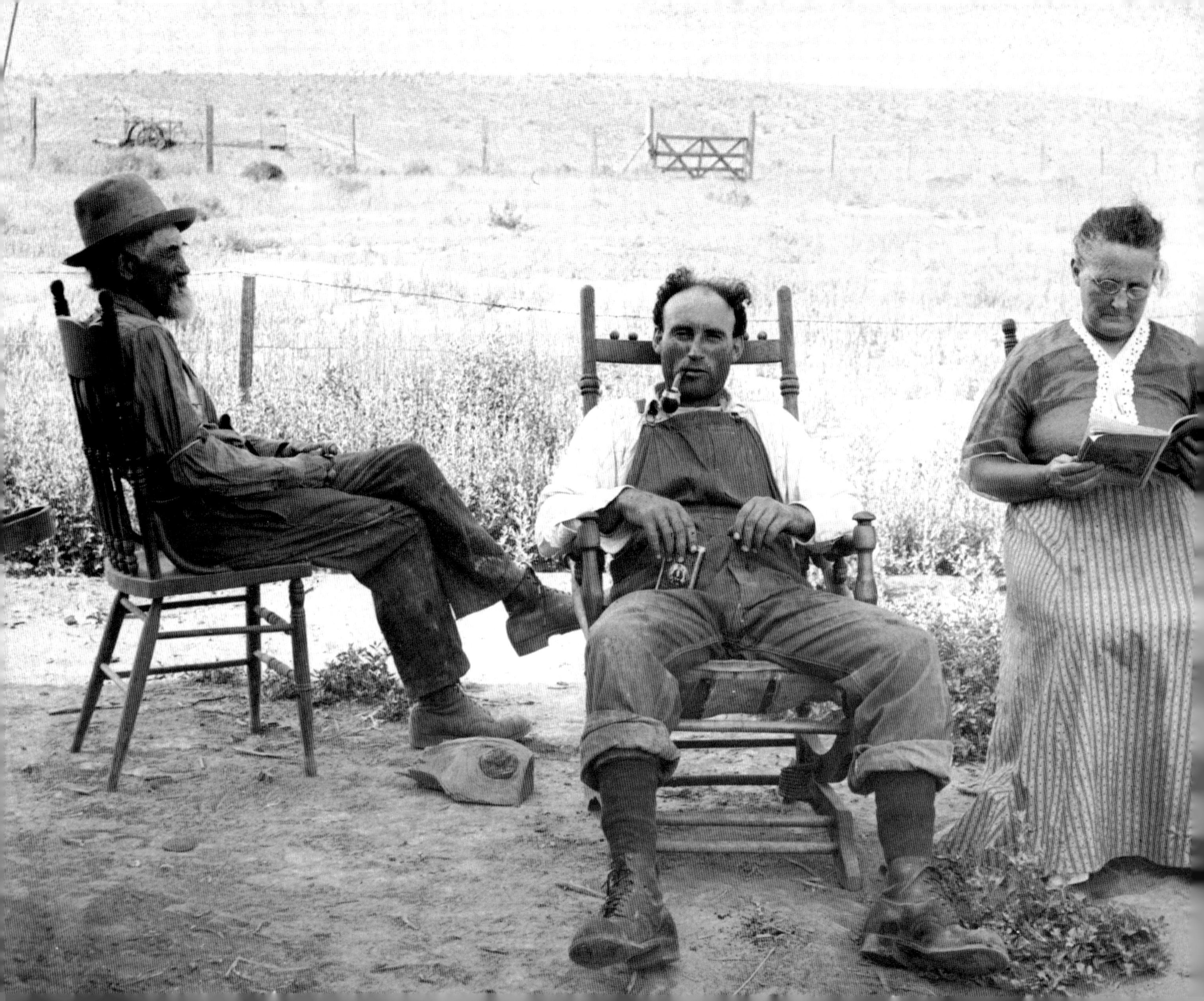

CHAPTER SEVEN
People of the Valley

What makes an area so special has less to do with its geography, transportation, businesses or schools than with its people. A place becomes extraordinary through its people's work ethic, philosophies, sense of honor and respect for others. What the Walla Walla Valley is today is due in large part to all those who by the sweat of their brow and perseverance laid the solid foundations upon which we build today. Those who carved out cities, farms and homes from a wilderness deserve more credit for our enviable quality of life than can ever be acknowledged.

Today we see the fruits of their labors and foresight. Buildings, streets, parks and schools bear the names of these individuals. Descendants of many of these early families are still here, a testament to the vitality and attraction of the area.

Left: Merry family members pose for the photograph on the homestead on Frog Hollow Road, Touchet-Lowden area, circa 1917. Pictured from left are, F.R. Merry, John Merry, and his wife Louisa Merry. *Photo courtesy John Merry*

Right: M.P. Groom family photo, 1885. The family homestead was in Huntsville. *Photo courtesy Richard Daniel*

Right: John "Jack" Ryan, circa 1878. *Photo courtesy Matthew Seeliger*

Far right: U.S. Army discharge papers for Private John Ryan, signed at Fort Walla Walla, May 4, 1884. *Photo courtesy Matthew Seeliger*

Below: Mary Gavin Ryan, circa 1878. *Photo courtesy Matthew Seeliger*

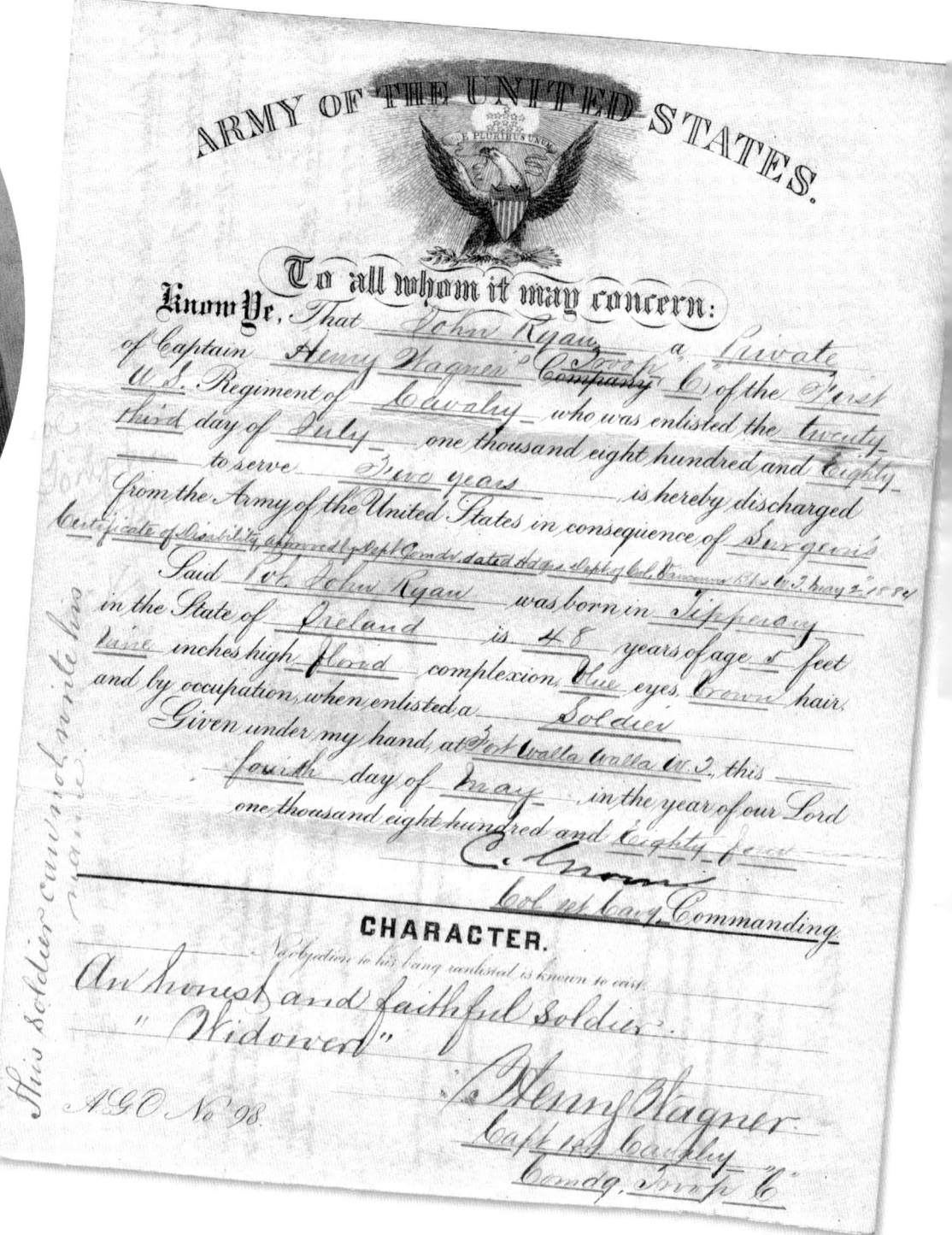

Left: Charles Stewart and Loretta Belle Wolfard Stewart, Colton, 1878.   *Photo courtesy Diane Jones*

Above: Wedding photo of William and Margaret (Ryan) Draper, circa 1882.
Photo courtesy Matthew Seeliger

Right: Goodman family photo, Walla Walla, 1883. Pictured, from left, William S. Goodman, his wife Irene Stewart Goodman, and Myrtle Goodman, his daughter.   *Photo courtesy Earl Stewart Blackaby*

Arthur Kibler's Mom Emma

Diane's Great Grandmother —

Joe Tompkins Mom

Above: Dr. Nelson Blalock, 1880. Dr. Nelson Blalock came to Walla Walla in 1872. In addition to his medical pursuits, he operated a successful wheat farm and orchard. He built a 28-mile long flume to move logs out of the Blue Mountains. In 1882 he donated 40 acres to Walla Walla College for their new school. Blalock also served as mayor of Walla Walla in 1889 and 1890.
Photo courtesy Fred L. Mitchell

Left: Wedding photo of Mary (McDonnell) Rorke and Jack Rorke, circa 1890. *Photo courtesy Charles Joe Tompkins*

Far Left: The McDonnell family, Walla Walla, circa 1888. Pictured, from left, standing, Edward, Alicia, Joseph, and Clement. Sitting, Emma, Stella, Mary and Leo. *Photo courtesy Charles Joe Tompkins*

Walla Walla Valley Memories

Above: Mayme Wilson (left) and Anne Caldwell Ivy, circa 1895. *Photo courtesy Fort Walla Walla Museum #87.38.2*

Left: Joseph and Alicia McDonnell, Walla Walla, circa 1880. *Photo courtesy Charles Joe Tompkins*

Left: William S. Goodman, Walla Walla, circa 1890. In 1875 Goodman purchased 400 acres of land and became one of the most successful sheep and stock men in the valley, raising fine Short-Horn cattle. *Photo courtesy Earl Stewart Blackaby*

Below: "Business card" showing William S. Goodman's herd taking the sweepstakes premium at the Walla Walla County Fair of 1880. *Photo courtesy Earl Stewart Blackaby*

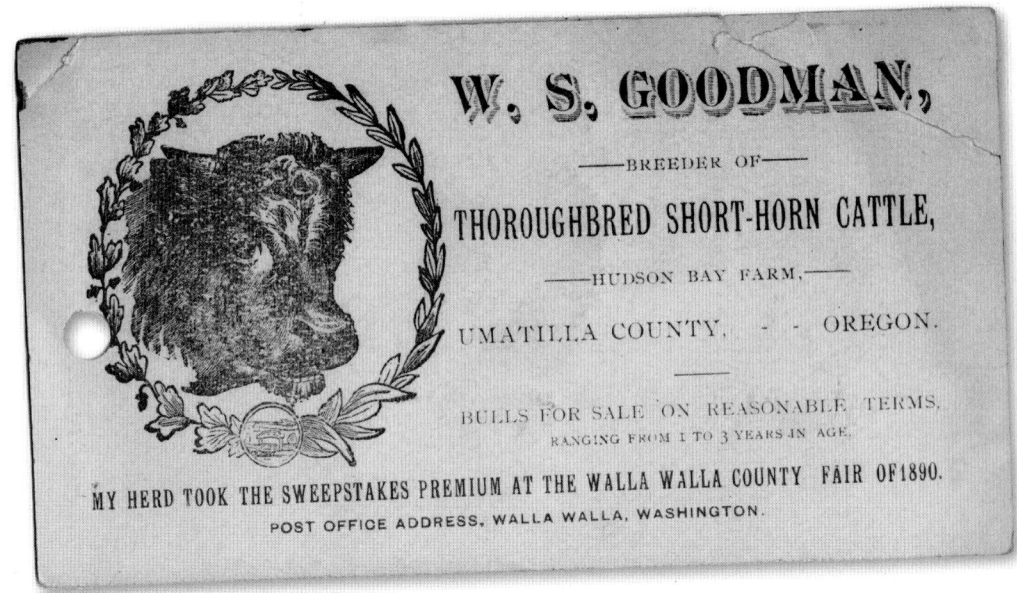

Left: The Damase Bergevin homestead, 1892. Pictured is Damase and his wife Mary Parmela and their children, Eleonie, who is on the horse behind her mother; Joseph is riding the other horse, Arthur Alexander is sitting on a chair between his parents and the twins, Clement Oliver and Clarence Chester are in a baby buggy. The two bottom plows were used to plow up the Virginia bunch grass hills to plant wheat. The horses are hitched to a rake that was to be used for raking wild hay for feeding the horses and cattle. The photo was taken about 3 miles east of Lowden on the south side of what is now highway 12, an area which to this day is referred to as Frenchtown because of the numerous French Settlers who came to the valley in the mid-1800s. *Photo courtesy Claro E. Bergevin*

Walla Walla Valley Memories

Right: Eunice and Gladys Reid doing the wash, Prescott, circa 1909. *Photo courtesy Dorothy Hall*

Far right: Siblings Guenn Snyder (front) and John Michael Peter Snyder on a bicycle in front of their house in Walla Walla, 1905. *Photo courtesy Karin Western*

Left: These young Walla Walla residents were known around town as the "Possum Gang." Photo circa 1907. *Photo courtesy Leontine Jaussaud Winn*

Right: The Pioneer Association meeting at Brussel's Grove, July 4, 1901. Included in the photo are: Dr. Nelson G. Blalock, Chief Bones, Mrs. Max Baumeister, Mary (Morris) Bussell, Mathias A. Caris, Sandy Cameron, Woodson Cummins, Amos Cummins, Martin Campbell, Ob Dewitt, America Dewitt, Andrew J. Evans, George Evans, Cantrell Frasier, Milton Evans, Charles Gregory, Will Hawley, Jo S. Harbert, Frank Harbert, H. H. Hungate, Mrs. H. H. Hungate, William Johnson, J.S. Jordan, Henry Jeffery, R. Kennedy, A.J. Lloyd, Professor W.D. Lyman, Frank Lowden Sr., C.C. Maiden, Mrs. Phelinda McKee, McAllister Lanna Margan, Will Nuttall, Hollon Parker, Mrs. Nancy E. Rice, Mrs. Philip Ritz, J.J. Rohn, Laura Shelton, Mrs. George Starrett, Louis Scholl, Mrs. Louis Scholl, Jap Scott, Mrs. Jap Scott, Mrs. Frank Villa, Nat Webb, A.C. Wellman, and Philander Witt.

Photo courtesy Fort Walla Walla Museum #UK.UK.5922

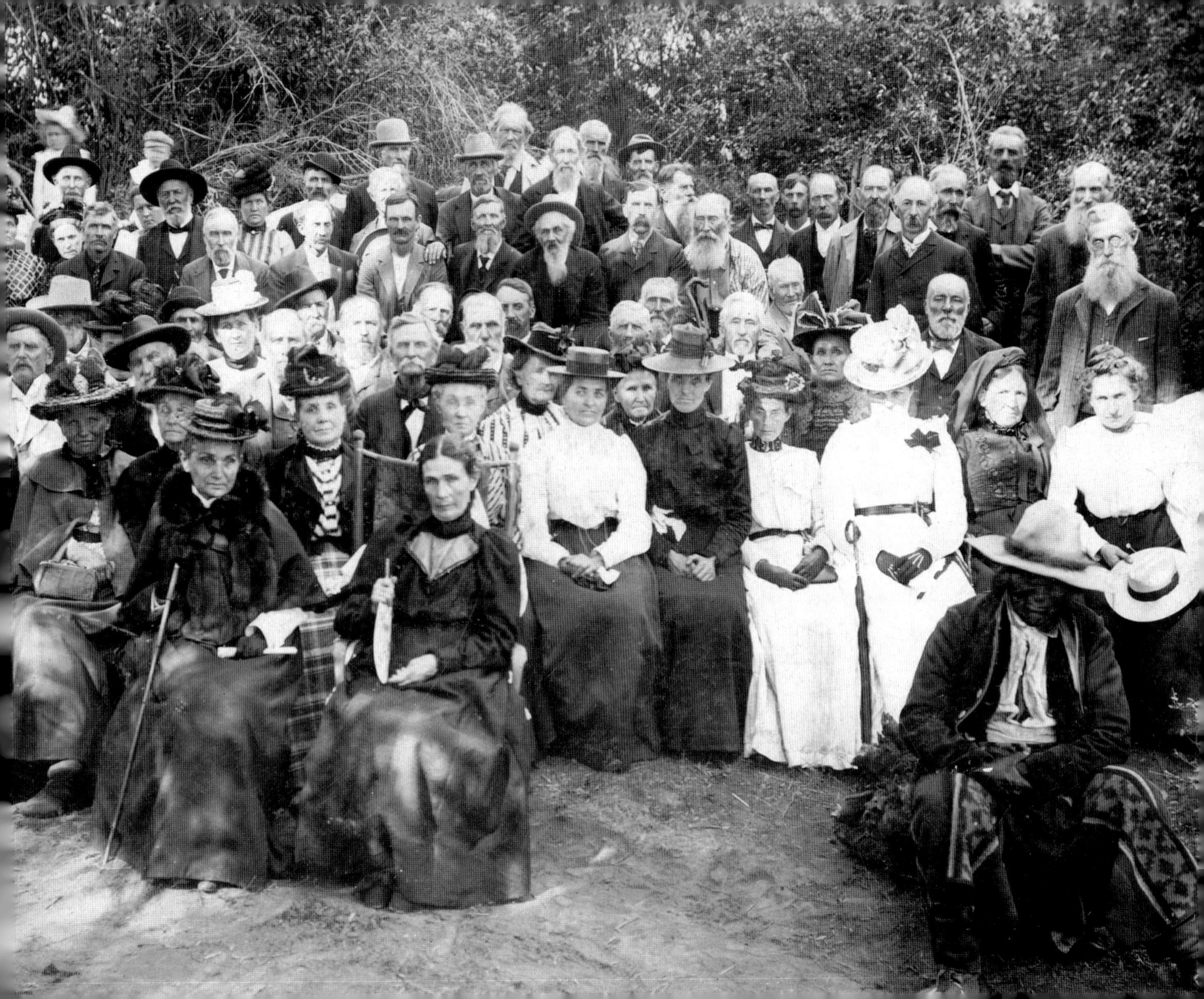

Right: Adolph Schwarz Jr. takes a ride on his mule, Walla Walla, circa 1910. *Photo courtesy Tracy Schwarz*

Above: Clyde H. McFaden of McFaden Photo Shop poses beside the old Walla Walla High School. *Photo courtesy Fred L. Mitchell*

Left: Benjamin R. Allen and his family in front of their home in Walla Walla, circa 1910. Also included in the photo is Benjamin's wife Ella Seeber Allen and their children Darl, Marie, and Marvin.

Photo courtesy Susan Queen

110   *People of the Valley*

Right: Saturno family, Walla Walla, circa 1910. Pictured, back row, Carmen Saturno and Giovaninni (Mrs. Nicholas) Saturno. Middle Row: Pasquale Saturno (born 1851 and died 1919), Mary (born 1849 and died 1916), and Josephine (daughter). The small child is Louise Saturno, daughter of Mr. & Mrs. Nicholas Saturno. Pasquale was the first row crop farmer/gardner in the valley in 1876. He was also the first commercial wine maker in the valley.

Photo courtesy Douglas Saturno

Above: Ruth Schwarz and Adolph Schwarz Jr. pose for the photograph in Walla Walla, circa 1910. *Photo courtesy Tracy Schwarz*

Left: The Charles A. Tompkins family, circa 1910. *Photo courtesy Charles Joe Tompkins*

Walla Walla Valley Memories

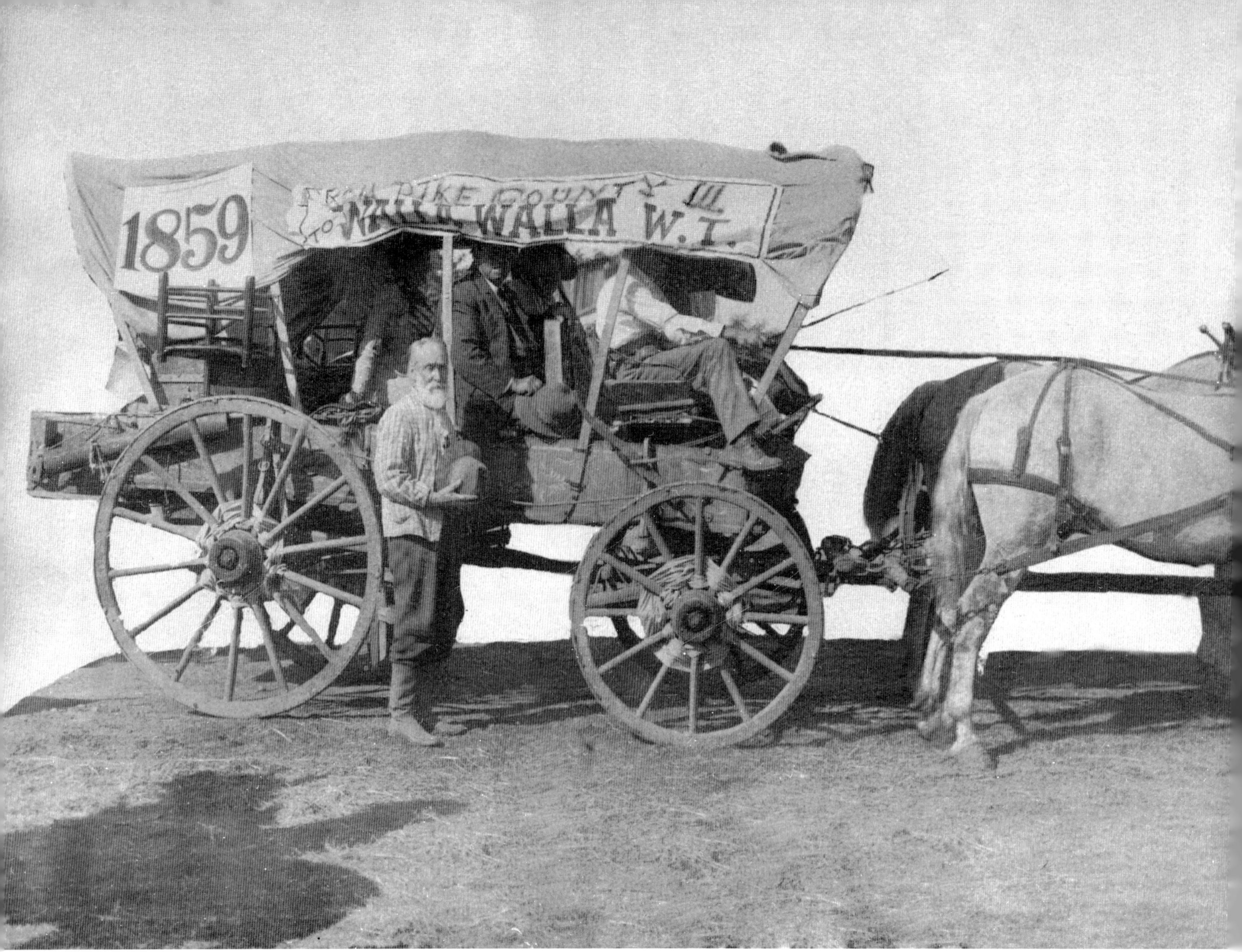
1859
PIKE COUNTY Ill
WALLA W.T.

Above: Siblings Marvin V. Allen and Marie K. Allen as Marvin is ready to go off to war, circa 1917. Marvin wore his WWI uniform and marched in every Veteran's Day Parade until his death in 1975. *Photo courtesy Susan Queen*

Left: Pasco Sam poses next to Wesley Lloyd and his son Tony, who is dressed in traditional Native American regalia. *Photo courtesy Fort Walla Walla Museum #05.20.253*

Far Left: William P. Winans and the immigrant wagon shown at Frontier Days in Walla Walla, circa 1915.
Photo courtesy Fred L. Mitchell

Walla Walla Valley Memories

Right: Edna Jackson, wife of Frank Jackson, shown with her Harley, Walla Walla, circa 1914. The family would attach side cars to each cycle, and with two kids and camping gear, they would head to the mountains for a weekend of camping. *Photo courtesy Jack Jackson*

Below: Family of Elder John T. Barnes (seated left) and Sarah Jane Parkes Barnes (seated right), in Touchet, circa 1915. Back row is identified from left as Lucy Ann, Fredrick, Josephine, Samuel, Rebecca, Edward and Edith.

Photo courtesy Judy Largent Treman

Above: Henry Clodius, Walla Walla, circa 1918.

Photo courtesy Tina (Clodius) Allington

People of the Valley

Left: Eunice Reid and Bill Reid churning butter at their home near Prescott, circa 1918. *Photo courtesy Dorothy Hall*

Above: John Yenney poses with his homemade wheelbarrow at the family home on Russell Creek, Walla Walla, 1919. *Photo courtesy Bert Yenney*

Right: The children of the Alie and Well McLean family pose on their horse in front of Green Park School on Clinton and Isaacs streets, Walla Walla, 1919. Pictured, from left, Margery, Gordon, and Eleanor. *Photo courtesy Robert Kibler family*

Walla Walla Valley Memories

Right: Mattie Coleman Cookerly, wife of John W. Cookerly with four of her grandchildren, John C. Tuttle (later Walla Walla Superior Court Judge), Madeline Cookerly Coryell, Dana Coleman Simmons Matthews, and Shirley Gardner Whitney Carey Hill, daughter of Ward Gardner, founder of Gardner's department store.
Photo courtesy Claire Coryell Siegel

Below: Fleenor children pose on Daisy and Snookums, Walla Walla, 1920. Pictured, from left, Ronal Marion, Homer Elmer, Verniece Gladys, Madge Dorcas and Clinton George. *Photo courtesy Richard Daniel*

Above: Four Giana sisters from Sacred Heart Orphanage in Walla Walla, circa 1919. The girls are identified as Francis, 8, Mary, 6, Rose, 5, and Camille, 4. *Photo courtesy Don Locati*

Below: Grandchildren of August and Sophia Lonneker at the City Park, later Pioneer Park, Walla Walla, circa 1923. Pictured, from left, Virginia Tarwater, Esther Taylor, Don Saxton, Ruth Saxton, Curtis Tarwater, Jessie Taylor and Gene Saxton. The City of Walla Walla hired August to plow the ground to develop the park around 1900, which is where this photo was taken. *Photo courtesy Vicki Ueckert*

Above: The Leon Jaussaud family in front of their home at 10th and Alder streets in Walla Walla, circa 1924. *Photo courtesy Leontine Jaussaud Winn*

Left: Patrick M. O'Brien, Walla Walla, 1925. *Photo courtesy Kathy O'Brien Henderson*

Above: Locati family members, pictured, left to right are Pierina Mainini Locati, Josephine Locati and Giuseppe Locati, Walla Walla, 1924. *Photo courtesy Marilyn McCann*

Right: Northern Italians take time from their July 4th, 1926, picnic to pose for the photographer near Mill Creek. Pictured, from left, back row, Ambrosina (Mrs. James) Locati, Giovinna (Mrs. Antonio) Zaro, James Locati, Mrs. Arbini, Caroline Arbini, Mrs. Buschini, Mrs. Bussini, Carlo Bossini (in hat), John Arbini, Mary (Mrs. John) Arbini. Middle row, Fred Locati (sitting), Pearl Buschini, Josephine Bossini, Caroline Zaro (Mrs. Earle) King, Agnes Zaro (Mrs. Joe) Spanish. First row, Remo Locati, Joe Zaro, Teresa Arbini, Mrs. Carlo Bossini, Louis Bossini, Carl Buschini, and Charles Zaro.
Photo courtesy Judy Jaquins

Walla Walla Valley Memories

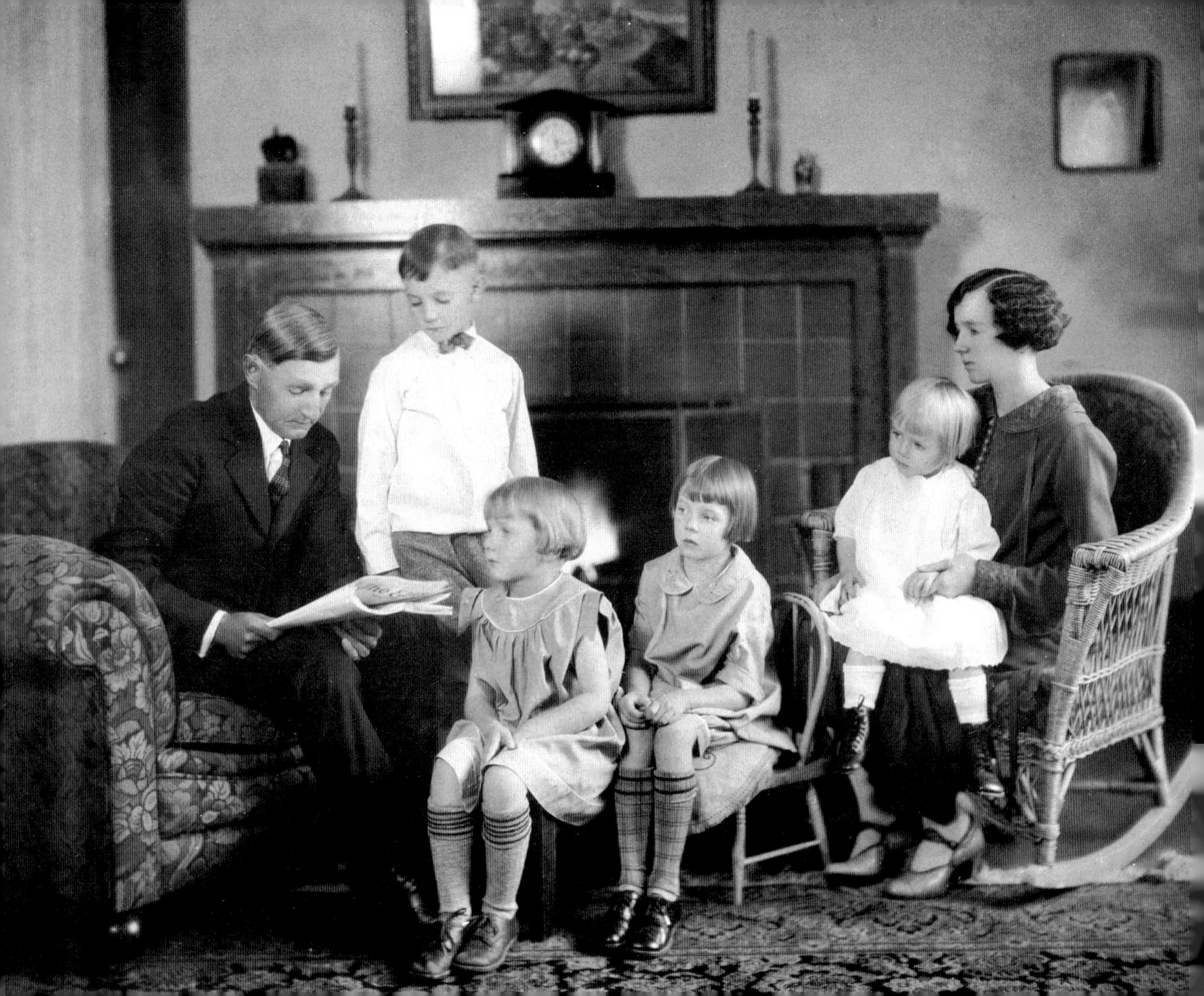

Above: Frank J. Jackson in front of Jackson's Sporting Goods, 25 West Main Street in Walla Walla, 1930. *Photo courtesy Fred L. Mitchell*

Left: The Paul Webb Sr. family, from left, Paul Webb, Sr., Paul Jr., Ruth, Mary Jane, Helen, and Minta Pettyjohn Webb, circa 1924. *Photo courtesy Paul Webb*

Left: Gladys Fleenor, Lydia Tricks, and Madge Fleenor pose in front of the post office in Walla Walla, 1929. *Photo courtesy Richard Daniel*

Below: Bob and Hazel Dix Harding at Pioneer Park in Walla Walla, circa 1929.

Photo courtesy Joyce and Darrel Martin

Walla Walla Valley Memories

Right: Fred Mitchell, Canadian Middleweight Boxing Champion, circa 1932. Mitchell was also the Pacific Coast Middleweight boxing champion. He coached wrestling and boxing at Walla Walla High School from 1935 through 1940 and his teams won championships every year. *Photo courtesy Fred L. Mitchell*

Above: Mollie and Nazaire E. Yelle, Walla Walla residents, all dressed up for the Whitman centennial celebration in 1936. *Photo courtesy Joe Drazan*

Left: Cecil Smith, George Bagley, Ben Colley, G.W. "Doc" Smith, and Charles Smith at Woodward Canyon Ranch at Lowden, circa 1935.

Photo courtesy Kathy Stritzel

Left: Walla Walla newlyweds Clarence Shaw and his new wife, Bessie, on their wedding day in 1936. The Shaws were local ranchers who owned Shawala Morgan Horse Ranch.
Photo courtesy Marie Batson

Far Left: Mary Robison Lynch on her favorite horse, Diploma, at her family's ranch in Walla Walla, circa 1936. She was also the Queen of the Pendleton Round-up in 1936. *Photo courtesy Margaret Lynch*

Below: Emmanuel and Salamina Frank, originally Germans from Russia, relocated from an Idaho dry farm to Walla Walla after the depression. The couple is shown with their five daughters, Mabel, Clara, Elenora, Agnes, and Alma, circa 1939. *Photo courtesy Marie Batson*

Walla Walla Valley Memories 121

Above: Geo. W. and Mabel Smith children riding Nubbins the horse, who was 20 years old, on the Ringhoffer Ranch in Lowden, 1936. Pictured, from left, Geo. (Pug), 14; Frances, 10; Lavonne, 18 months; Lilly, 8; Louise, 5; Grace, 7; Shari, 2 months; Margie, 12; and Elmer, 13. *Photo courtesy Geo. W. and Mabel Smith family, Shari Richmond and Frances Wright*

Above: Jim Huie, owner of Huie's Furniture and Appliance, harvesting lettuce on his father's farm located on the current site of Walla Walla General Hospital, circa 1939.
Photo courtesy Marty Huie

Right: Faye Huie and her children, Anthony and Beverly, in Walla Walla.
Photo courtesy Marty Huie

Below: J.J. (Jake) Lucinger holding Jack Jackson (left), and Ginger Jackson, daughter of Harold Jackson, in front of Jackson's Sporting Goods, Walla Walla, July 4, 1938. Lucinger was the area's only locksmith. His shop was located in the back of Jackson's. He operated his shop at that location from 1925-1955. *Photo courtesy Jack Jackson*

Walla Walla Valley Memories

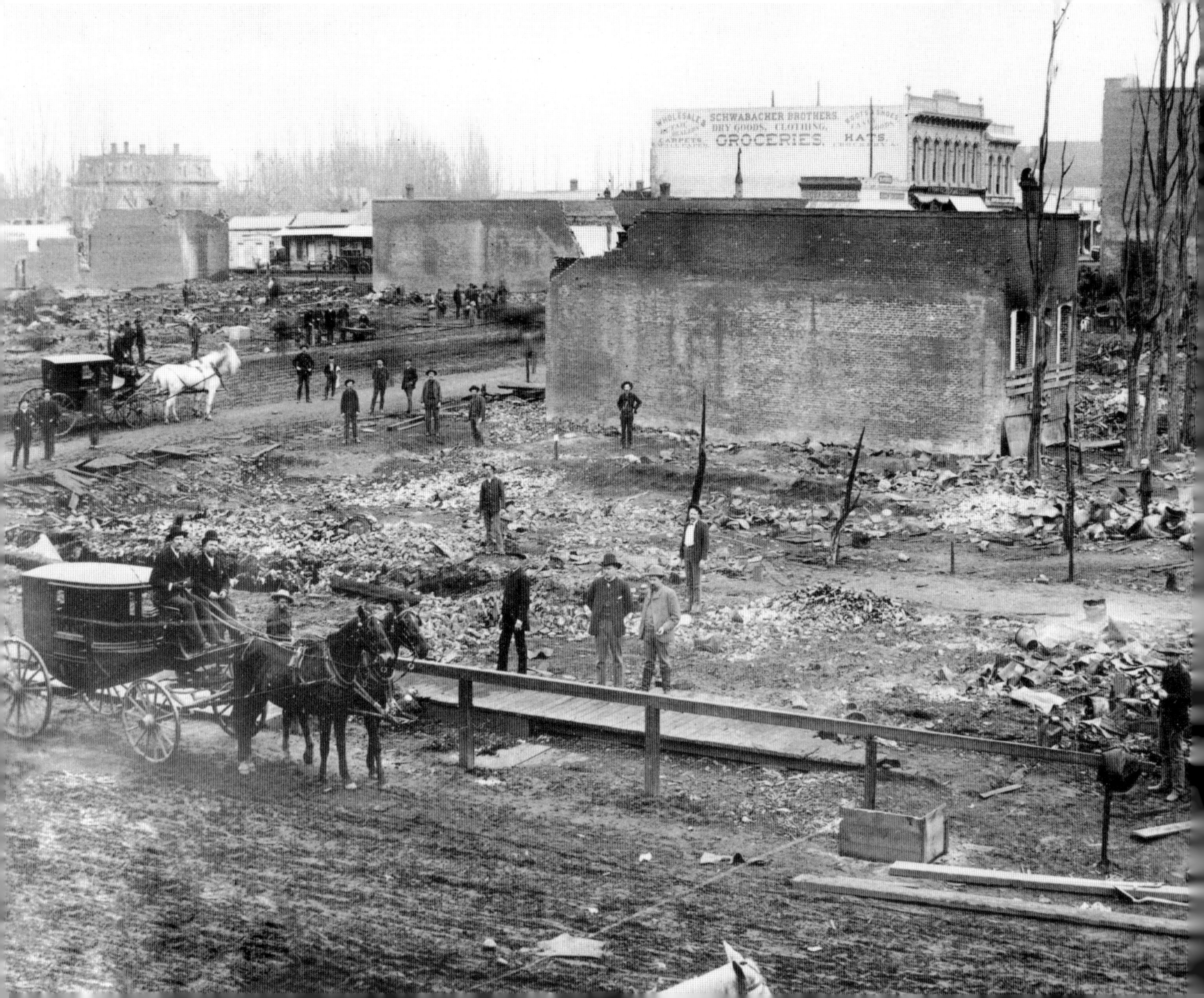
SCHWABACHER BROTHERS
GROCERIES.
HATS

CHAPTER EIGHT
Disaster Strikes

Things do not always go smoothly in people's lives or in the lives of their communities. The whims of Mother Nature or the ravages of an unchecked fire can bring about hard times. The Walla Walla Valley is no stranger to hardships. Too often over the years, fires reduced large sections of communities or special structures to ash and rubble. But people would rebuild.

Floods have flashed through the area, inundating streets, homes, and businesses with cold, muddy waters. One of the worst on record was in 1931. The aftermath left communities looking like a war zone. But people would rebuild.

Snowstorms haven't been as devastating as the fires or floods, but they have taken their toll. On Jan. 31, 1916, 48 inches of snow buried Walla Walla and other areas in the Valley. But people immediately began digging out and soon found ways to cope and to go on with their daily lives.

The inner strength of local residents was tested and tempered time and time again by these disasters and a flu pandemic. Each time they proved their mettle.

Left: Aftermath of the greatest fire in Walla Walla's history, May 7, 1887. This view is from the balcony of the Stine House, looking east, with 4th Street in the foreground. *Photo courtesy Francis Christiano*

Right: Overturned train cars lay in the mud off the tracks after the railway wreck at Mud Creek in 1906. *Photo courtesy Fort Walla Walla Museum #UK.UK.191*

Above: A significant amount of downtown Walla Walla burned March 7, 1887. *Photo courtesy Fort Walla Walla Museum #83.19.78*

Left: The March 7, 1887 fire in Walla Walla. *Photo courtesy Fred L. Mitchell*

Right & Far Right: The Jones Building fire (A.M. Jensen Store) at the corner of Alder and 2nd streets in Walla Walla that took the life of Assistant Chief Wolf, January 26, 1912.
Photo courtesy Fred L. Mitchell

Left: St. Mary's Hospital fire, Walla Walla, January 27, 1915. *Photo courtesy Fred L. Mitchell*

Below: East Alder Street after 48" of snow fell on Walla Walla in 1916. *Photo courtesy Fred L. Mitchell*

Above: Heavy snow in front of the Pacific Telephone and Telegraph Company in Walla Walla after the big storm of 1916. *Photo courtesy Leontine Jaussaud Winn*

Right: A wreck on the Oregon Washington Railroad & Navigation line, April 15, 1912. *Photo courtesy Fort Walla Walla Museum #92.67.2*

Walla Walla Valley Memories

127

Left: Snow piled up in front of the Book Nook during the 1916 snowstorm in Walla Walla. *Photo courtesy Fred L. Mitchell*

Far left: A view of Main Street, looking east from between 2nd and 3rd streets in Walla Walla after the great snowstorm of 1916. *Photo courtesy Francis Christiano*

Below: Aftermath of a heavy snowstorm in Walla Walla, where 48" of snow fell, January 31, 1916. This is a view of Main Street, looking east, from between 3rd and 4th streets. *Photo courtesy Fred L. Mitchell*

Above: The south side of Main Street looking west, from Colville Street, during the 1931 flood in Walla Walla. *Photo courtesy Fred L. Mitchell*

Right: A Walla Walla resident climbs a pole to escape the fast rising waters at the corner of Second and Birch streets, April 1931. *Photo courtesy Fred L. Mitchell*

Far Right: Looking east on Alder from between 2nd and 1st streets, April 1931. *Photo courtesy Ginger Kelly*

Below: Floodwaters rise during the 1931 flood in Dayton. *Photo courtesy Fred L. Mitchell*

SALES AND SERVICE
CLAUDE NEON SIGNS
DeLaval
TIRES
PUNCH GARAGE
STORAGE
THE FAIR
STORAGE
TELEPHONE

Above: Flooding in Walla Walla, April 1931. *Photo courtesy Ginger Kelly*

Left: An automobile tries to navigate the floodwaters at 2nd and Alder streets during the 1931 flood in Walla Walla. *Photo courtesy Gary and Carolee Armstrong*

Above: The 1931 flood in Walla Walla. *Photo courtesy Janet Headley*

Right: City folks are using the pumper to pump out basements after the 1931 flood in Walla Walla. *Photo courtesy Fred L. Mitchell*

Disaster Strikes

Above: Wildwood Park at Division and Boyer streets in Walla Walla during the big flood of 1931. *Photo courtesy Phyllis Teal*

Above: Flooding on Birch Street in Walla Walla, April 1931. The Birchway Apartments are on the left.
Photo courtesy Phyllis Teal

Right: Streets and sidewalks are washed away during the 1931 flood in Walla Walla. This view is looking north on Palouse from Birch Street. *Photo courtesy Gary and Carolee Armstrong*

Walla Walla Valley Memories 133

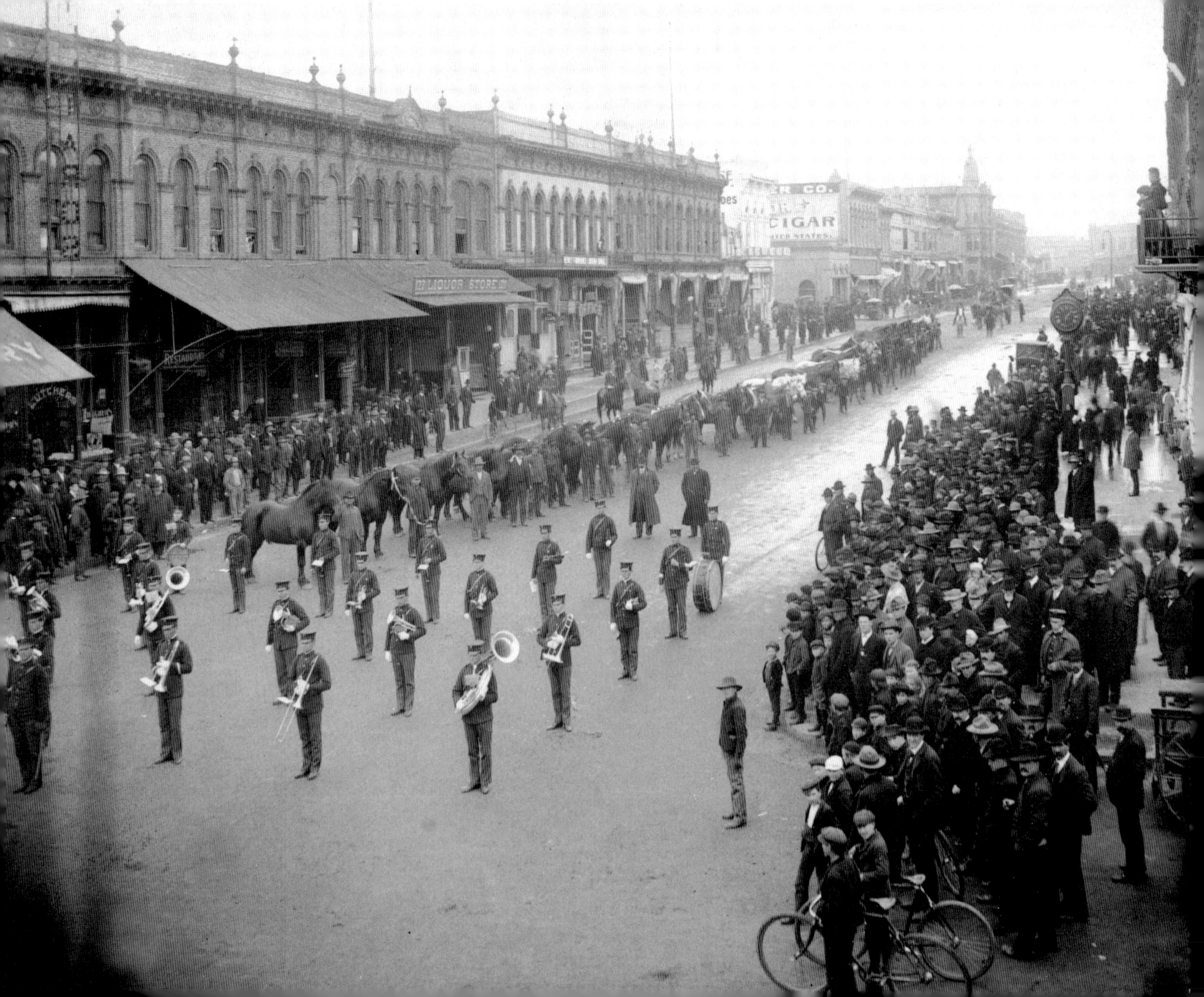

122 LIQUOR STORE 122
CIGAR

CHAPTER NINE
Recreation & Celebration

All work and no play ... just wouldn't be the Walla Walla Valley. Area residents played as hard as they worked. Sometimes they found ways to combine the two through rodeo events or festivals celebrating different harvests. Hunting and fishing were popular diversions that had the added benefit of putting food on the table. Picnics, especially for the Fourth of July or reunions, were an opportunity for celebration and for family and friends to share some time together.

Sports teams have been a staple of the area with baseball games played at such diverse locations as Fort Walla Walla and the Washington State Penitentiary. When things would get too hot, people could always go swimming.

Every occasion in the Valley seemed to call for a parade; among the biggest were those promoting fairs. The fairs also meant horse racing, another popular pastime.

The arts community already had a strong presence throughout the area, staging many plays and performances by musical groups.

Left: Walla Walla Concert Band in a horse parade down Main Street, as seen from 4th Street, looking east, Walla Walla, circa 1908. *Photo courtesy Fort Walla Walla Museum #87.15.15*

Right: Local men's singing group, circa 1892. The piano player for this group was Cara Yatta Manhard (Mrs. Harry Gilbert). *Photo courtesy Janet Headley*

Above: Yakama Canutt, well-known rodeo personality, bulldogging at Walla Walla Frontier Days in the early 1900s.
Photo courtesy Fred L. Mitchell

Right: Tex McLeod, World Champion fancy roper during Frontier Days in Walla Walla, early 1900s.
Photo courtesy Fred L. Mitchell

Far Right: Ezra Meeker, wagon and oxen leading the 1908 fair parade in Walla Walla after his Puyallup to Washington DC wagon trip in 1906-07.
Photo courtesy Fort Walla Walla Museum
#93.155.172

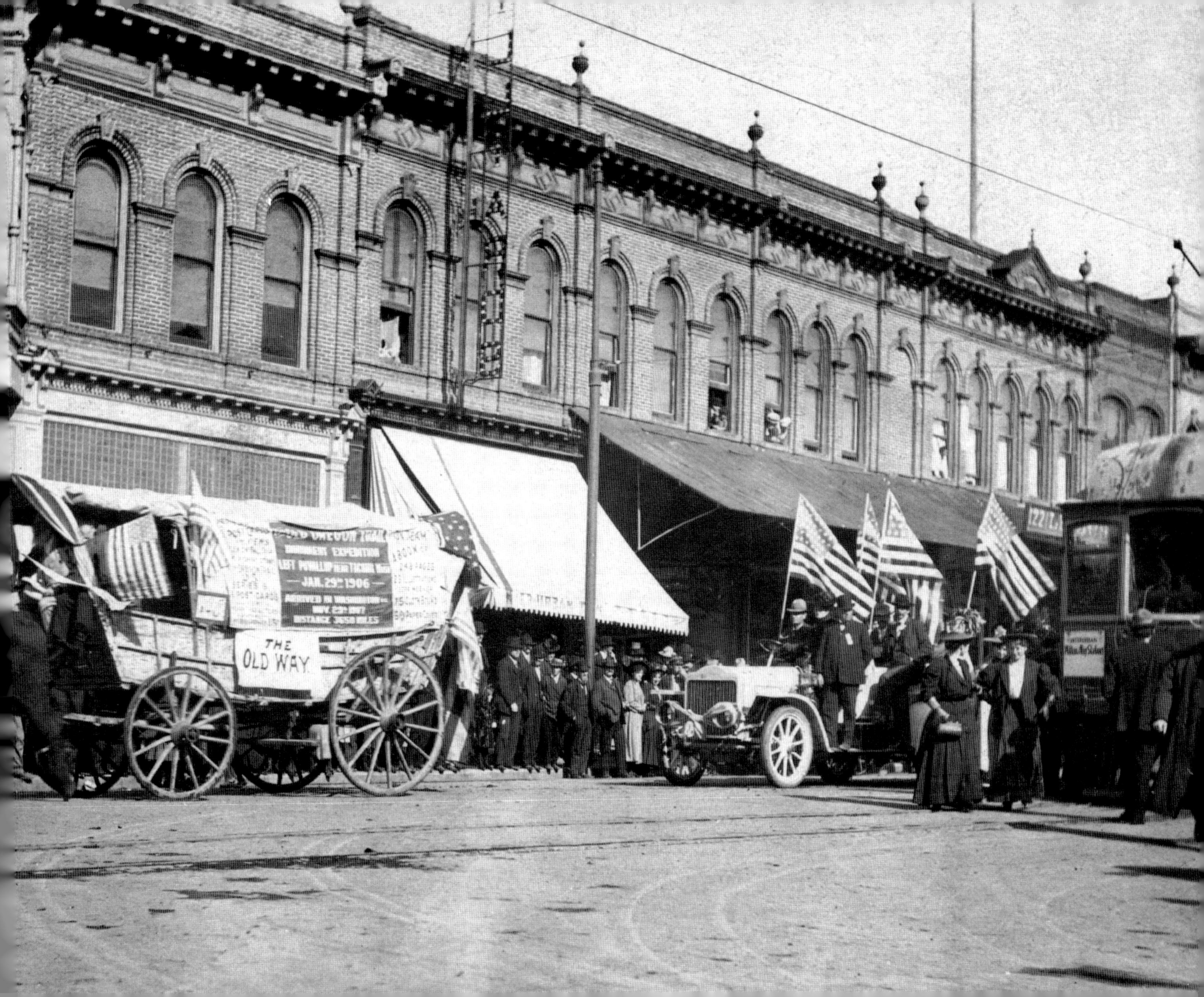

EXPEDITION
JAN. 29th 1906
DISTANCE 3650 MILES
THE OLD WAY

Right: Walla Walla Frontier Days, 1906.
Photo courtesy Fred L. Mitchell

Above: Food booth at Walla Walla Frontier Days, 1906.
Photo courtesy Fred L. Mitchell

Left: Walla Walla Frontier Days, 1906. *Photo courtesy Fred L. Mitchell*

Recreation & Celebration

Above: Horses and riders gather on North Main Street during Waitsburg's sixth annual horse show, May 1, 1909. *Photo courtesy Henry V. "Bill" Zuger*

Above left: Crowd gathers on Alder Street for one of the frequent parades in Walla Walla, early 1900s. *Photo courtesy Fred L. Mitchell*

Left: Walla Walla dignitaries greet President Taft when he visits Walla Walla, October 7, 1911. It was a two-hour visit, hosted by Gov. Hay and Sen. Levi Ankeny. *Photo courtesy Fred L. Mitchell*

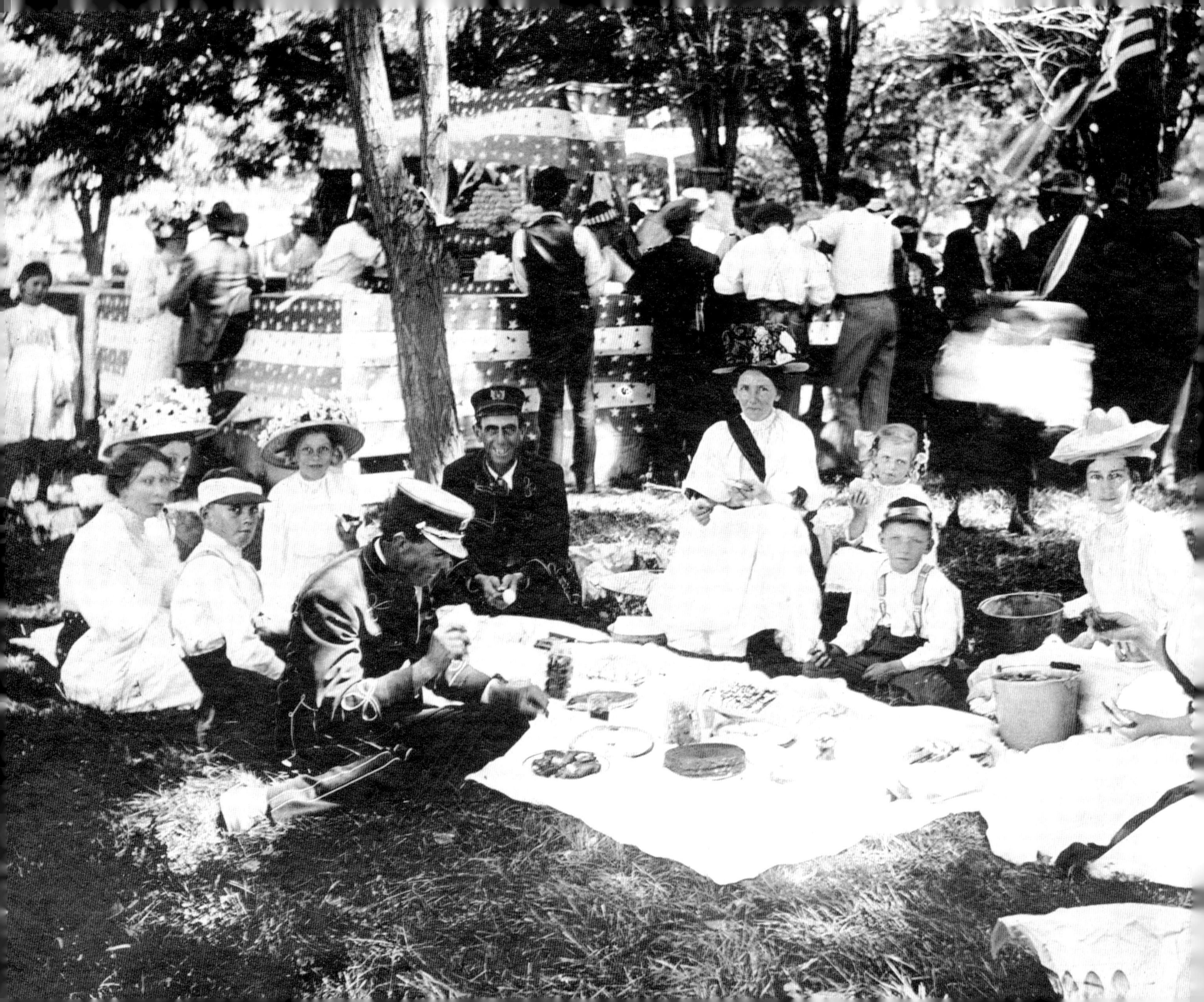

Left: Fourth of July celebration in Touchet, circa 1909. Seated around the picnic blanket from left are: Lottie Barnes, Dola Jackson, Josephine Barnes, Mr. Hammond, Jesse Weathers, Anna Weathers, Lou Weathers, unidentified, and Mrs. Hammond. Dolph Weathers is in front between Dola and Josephine. *Photo courtesy Judy Largent Treman*

Right: Royal Neighbors float in a Touchet 4th of July parade in 1909. The only three people identified in the photo are Mollie Payne, Mrs. E.K. Huber, and Anna Weathers. *Photo courtesy Judy Largent Treman*

Above: Apple Harvest celebration in Freewater, Oregon, 1909. *Photo courtesy Judy Largent Treman*

Left: Fishing and beer exhibition, circa 1910. Vasco Smith, Chas. Martin, Guy York, Art Harris, Charles McKean, Wm. VanDeWater, and Jack Masey. *Photo courtesy Fred L. Mitchell*

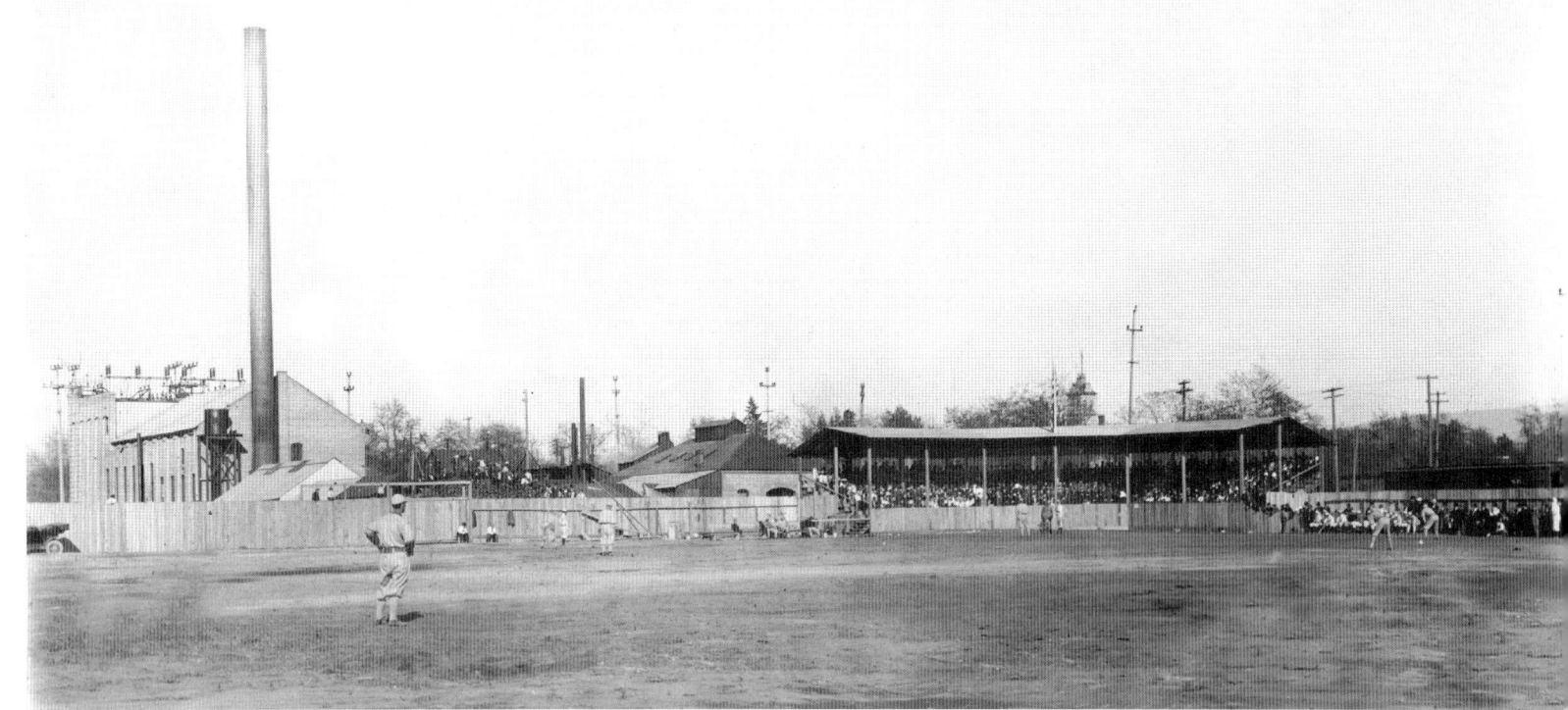

Right: Sportsman Park, early baseball field in Walla Walla, circa 1910. This ballpark was located on the north side of Rose Street, east of 9th Street.
Photo courtesy Fred L. Mitchell

Above: Horse race at the fairgrounds in Walla Walla, circa 1910.
Photo courtesy Francis Christiano

Left: Italian-Americans Tony Locati and Mike Curcio, on horses, lead a parade down Main Street in Walla Walla on Columbus Day, 1911. This view down Main Street is looking east from 3rd Street. *Photo courtesy Francis Christiano*

Recreation & Celebration

Left: Dedication of the Christopher Columbus statue on the front lawn of the Walla Walla County Courthouse, October 12, 1911. The celebration took place because for the first time Columbus Day was declared by the legislature to be a Washington State legal holiday. Chairman of the proceedings was the Hon. W.H. Dunph, and other dignitaries included: Mayor A.J. Gillis, orator of the day Rev. J.D. O'Brien, Rev. Luigi Roccati of Gonzaga College, J.N. McCaw, ex-senator Levi Ankeny, Father Van de Van of St. Patrick's Catholic Church, Captain Ross and Lieutenants Holm and McCoy of Compay K, Mr. and Mrs. Frank Yuse, Joseph Tachi, Robert Salatino, and Emilio Guglielmelli, secretary of the Italian committee. The statue and pedestal, costing over $1,000 at the time, were donated by nearly 100 contributors from the Walla Walla Italian colony, which also contributed $75 for the large silk Italian flag. Preceding the dedication ceremonies there was a large parade headed by Italian drummers, followed by Grand Marshall Tony Locati and aide Mike Curcio mounted on horses; a platoon of Walla Walla police in old-style London "bobbie" hats led by Chief Mike Davis, members of the fire department, the Walla Walla band, and members of the Columbus Day committee and the Italian colony in a long line of cabs. City offices were closed for the occassion, as were banks and many businesses. Schools were also let out early for the celebration. *Photo courtesy Fort Walla Walla Museum #UK.UK.8294*

Above: Horse race during Frontier Days, circa 1912.
Photo courtesy Lucille Whitman

Right: Chariot race during Frontier Days in 1912.
Photo courtesy Lucille Whitman

Walla Walla Valley Memories

Right: Maroney at the Frontier Days in Walla Walla, early 1900s. *Photo courtesy Fort Walla Walla Museum #96.32.13*

Below right: War Dance during Walla Walla Frontier Days, 1913. *Photo courtesy Fred L. Mitchell*

Below: Umatilla Indians during Frontier Days in Walla Walla, 1913. The Elks building can be seen in the background at the northwest corner of 4th and Alder streets. *Photo courtesy Fred L. Mitchell*

Recreation & Celebration

Left: The Pioneers Reunion in front of Reynolds Hall on the Whitman College campus in Walla Walla, 1915.

Photo courtesy Fort Walla Walla Museum #92.69.1

Below: Native Americans on parade during Frontier Days, circa 1914. In the background is the south side of Main Street, between 2nd and 3rd streets.

Photo courtesy Fred L. Mitchell

Above: Walla-Walla County Fair Association's "Better Baby" contest in 1914. The entrants in the contest ranged from 7 months old to 5 years old. Pictured are: Mary Charlotte Brewer, Elva Robberson, Arline Robberson, Marjorie Stirling, Martha Jane Hottel, Eleanor Alice McLean, Samuel Nesbin, Donald Froenske, Donald Baird, Harold Doll, Loren Steward, Joseph Kalisky, Wallace Davis, Forest Onriegs, Atta Marie Warren, Margaret Johnson, Jean Summers, and Gerald Bird.

Photo courtesy Fort Walla Walla Museum #80.7.1

Above: Baseball game at the State Penitentiary, Walla Walla, early 1900s.
Photo courtesy Fred L. Mitchell

Right: St. Francis Catholic Church dedication, Walla Walla, circa 1915.
Photo courtesy Douglas Saturno

Far Right: Horse show and strawberry festival in Milton-Freewater, 1915. Jess York is standing next to his sons, Grant (in wagon), Dillard and Ranzy (walking behind). Jess York was originally from North Carolina, but raised his family on his large wheat ranch between Weston and Milton-Freewater.
Photo courtesy Bonnie York Stephens

148

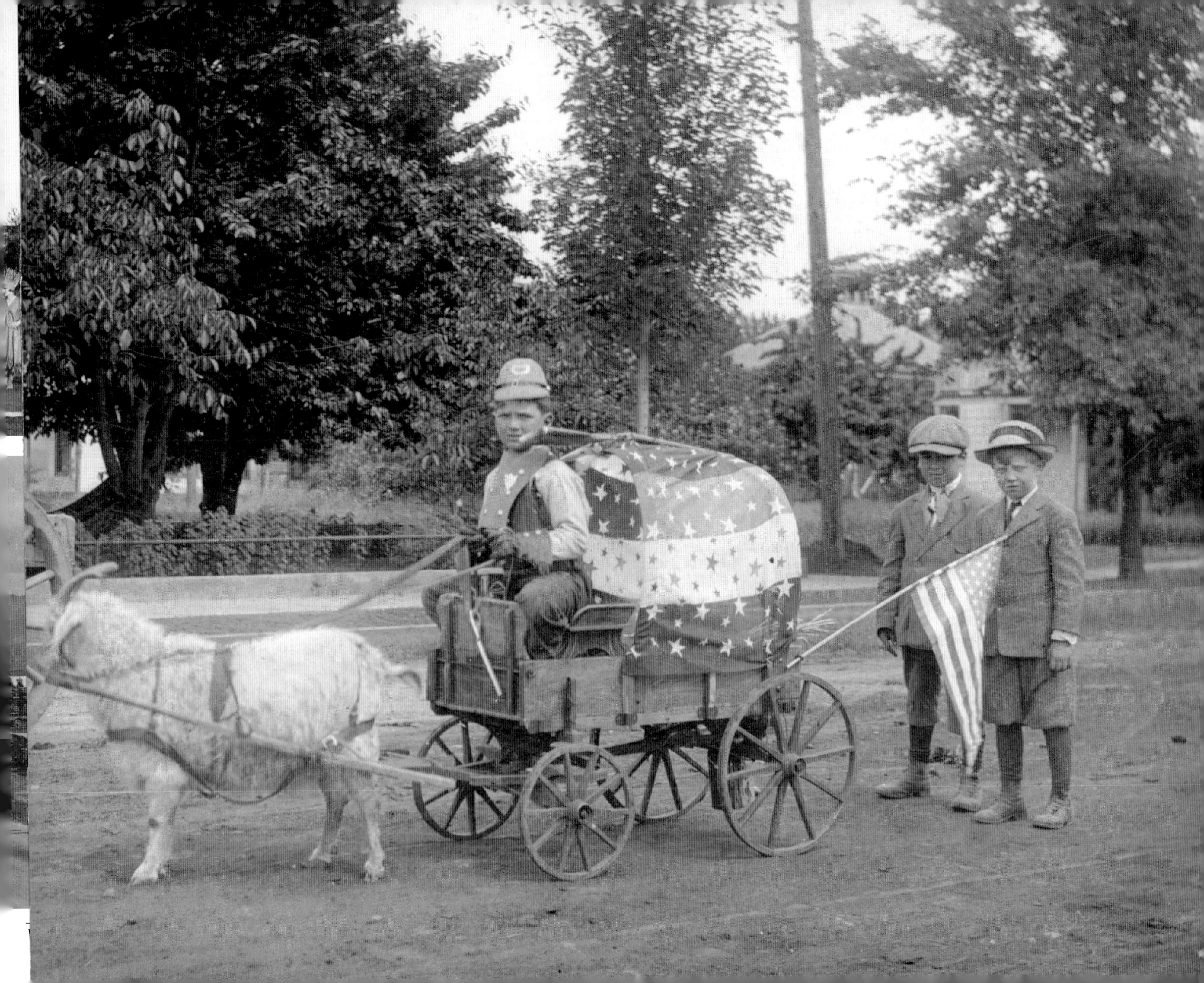

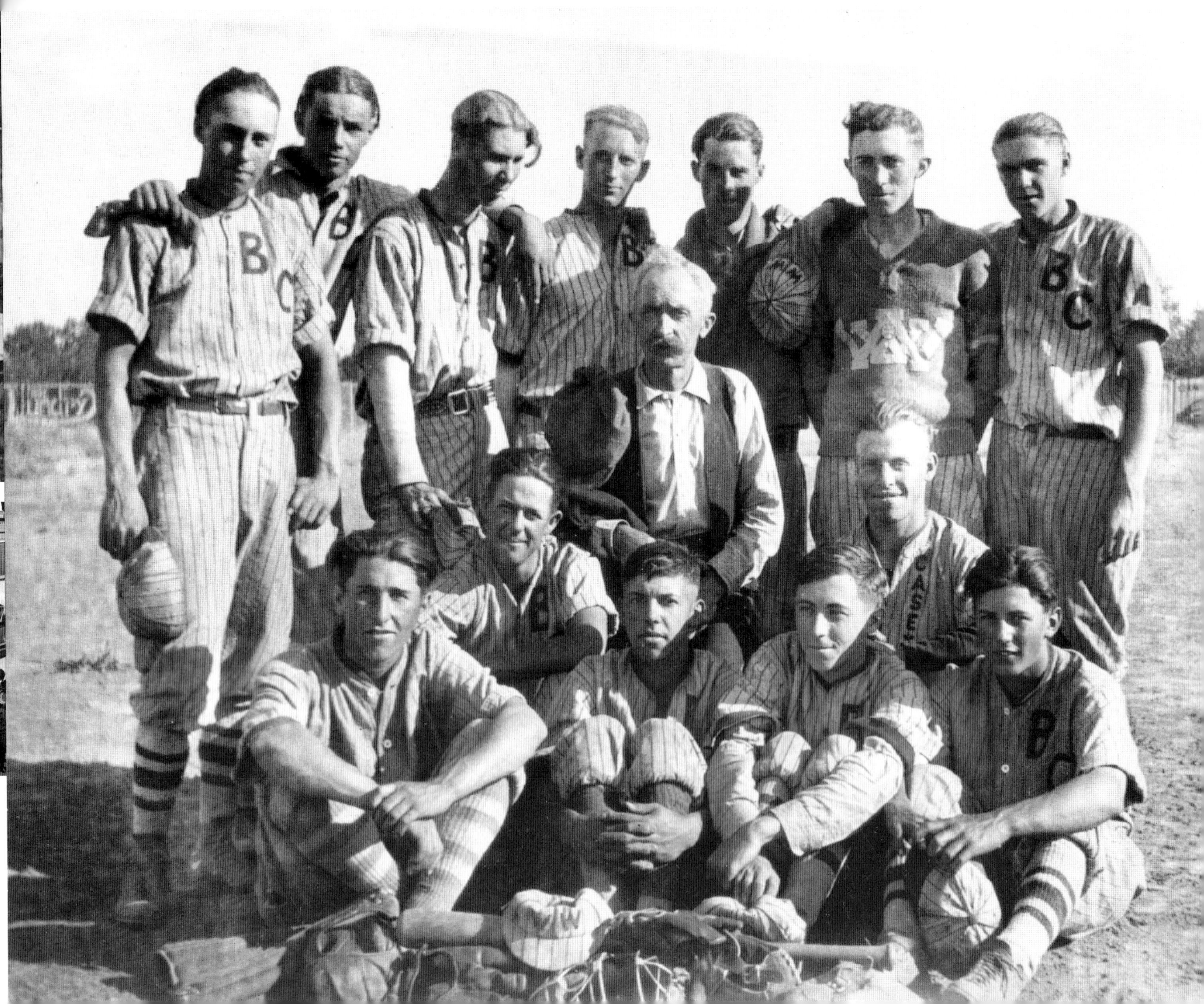

Left: The Bearcats baseball team, 1923. The Bearcats won the valley championship in Freewater, Oregon in 1923. They also won it in 1924 and 1925. Included on the team were: Howard Stockdale, Sheik Cummings, Claude Wetzel, Kenneth Owsley, Francis Witt, Robert Summers, Dan LaClair, Tommy Gardner, John Summers, Francis Cunnington, Armand Davin, Jake Cunnington, Howard Summers, and Brownie O'Hair.

Photo courtesy Fort Walla Walla Museum #86.29.1

Right: Members of the Walla Walla I.O.O.F. Grand Lodge in formation, June 6, 1923. *Photo courtesy Fred L. Mitchell*

Above: Mill Creek Farm Bureau presents the play, "When a Feller Needs a Friend" at Mill Creek Hall in Touchet, circa 1928. The players are identified from left as Ralph Danielson, Blanche Danielson, Ruth Gilkerson, Cliff Task, Irene Gilkerson Davis, Mr. Anderson, Genevieve Gilkerson Ferrel, Lee Gilkerson, Gilbert Thomas, and Mrs. Anderson. *Photo courtesy Judy Largent Treman*

Left: Milton-Freewater 1st Christian Church convention in 1924. *Photo courtesy Shirley Dickerson*

Walla Walla Valley Memories

Above: May Day Festival, Walla Walla, 1923.
Photo courtesy Fred L. Mitchell

Right: The largest buck of the season is on display in front of Jackson's Sporting Goods in Walla Walla, circa 1935. Pictured, from left, Bert Smith, Charles Parker, and Stella Parker. This buck would win a prize at the end of the season.
Photo courtesy Jack Jackson

Far Right: Crowd gathers to "watch" the World Series in front of the Evening and Sunday Morning Bulletin, south side of Alder street, between 1st and 2nd streets, Walla Walla, circa 1929. The Casper's building, at right, is where McFaden did his auto demonstration 13 years earlier (page 151). *Photo courtesy Douglas Saturno*

Below: Ralph Jackson, right, displays his fish that were caught in the Tucannan River, circa 1930. The man on the left was the piano player at the Liberty Theater when silent movies were shown.
Photo courtesy Jack Jackson

154   *Recreation & Celebration*

CASPER'S
BULLETIN
TAYLOR
RASMUSSENS
HARDWARE
THE GRAND
BILLIAR
PARLOR
GRAND

Recreation & Celebration

Above: Walla Walla College float during Whitman's Centennial parade August 13-16, 1936.
Photo courtesy Dorlin and Judy Haste

Above: Agnes and Clinton Cote and baby Annette, dressed to celebrate the Whitman Centennial in 1936.
Photo courtesy Marie Batson

Left: Whitman Centennial Parade, Walla Walla, August 13-16, 1936.
Photo courtesy Fred L. Mitchell

Right: An entry passes by the Liberty Theater on East Main Street during the Centennial Parade, Walla Walla, August 13-16, 1936. *Photo courtesy Claire Coryell Siegel*

Walla Walla Valley Memories

Index

1st Battalion, Company I, 84–85
4th Calvalry, 88
14th Cavalry, 93, 137
146th Artillery, Battery A, 96–97

Abbot, Frank, 137
Abbot Stage line, 34
Adams, Roy, 150
Adkins, Thomas A., 24
agriculture, about, 19
Allen, Benjamin R., and family, 110
Allen, Marie K., 113
Allen, Marvin V., 113
Anderson, Betty, 82
Anderson, L.F., 63
Anderson, Luetta, 82
Anderson, Merrill, 21
Anderson, Mr. and Mrs., 153
Angell, Audrey, 82
Angell, Robert, 82
Ankney, Charity, 65
Ankney, Harriett Lalle, 65
Appling, Ella Mae, 82
Arbini, Caroline, 117
Arbini, John, 117
Arbini, Mary, 117
Arbini, Mrs., 117
Arbini, Teresa, 117
Archer, Jack, 29
Archer, Rhodes, 29
Armstrong, Miriam, 82
Arnold, J.J. "Jake," 61
Auker, Ruth, 82–83

Bagley, George, 120
Bailry, Leonore, 67
Baird, Donald, 147
Baker, Frank, 61
Baker, Howard, 65
Baker School, 62–63, 79
Baldwin, Art, 29
Baldwin, Bill, 29
Barnes, John T., and family, 114
Barnes, Josephine, 143
Barnes, J.T., 52

Barnes, Lottie, 143
Barnes, Sam, 32–33
Barrett, Annie, 67
Bastron, LeRoy, 81
Baumeister, Mrs. Max, 108–9
Bayer, Arthur, 65
Bayer, Isabelle, 65
Bearcats baseball team, 152
Beatty, Franklin, 66
Beaver, Bill, 74
Beaver, Reinard, 74
Beck, Ruth, 66
Beck, Stanley, 82
Becker, Flora J., 82
Bender, L.A., 82–83
Bender, W.H., 86
Bennett, Mrs. Mamie L., 61
Berg, Charles, 92
Berg, Horace, 74–75
Berger, Ray, 21
Bergevin, Chas., 21
Bergevin, Clarence, 31
Bergevin, Clem, 21, 31
Berney, Evan, 74
Berney School, 72, 74
Berry, Leta, 74
Berryman, Chester, 48
Biagi, Wilburt, 82
Biersner, Blanche, 74
Biersner, Myrtle, 66
Bird, Gerald, 147
Bishop, Roberta, 82
Blalock, Nelson, 103, 108–9
Blalock, Yancy, 85, 106
Bones, Chief, 108–9
Bossini, Josephine, 117
Bossini, Louis, 117
Bossini, Mr. and Mrs. Carlo, 117
Bowman, Fred, 68
Boyd, Lee, 76
Boyer, Margaret, 65
Braden School, 64
Bradford, Doris, 82
Bradford, Mildred, 82
Brashear, Dorothy Jackson, 41

Bratton, W.A., 63
Brents, Helen, 65
Brewer, Mary Charlotte, 147
Britton, R. L., 39
Britton, Louise Jaussaud, 39
Brock, Stanley, 66
Brown, Alberta L., 82
Brown, B.H., 63
Brown, Carrie, 82–83
Brunton, Fred, 68
Brussel's Grove, 108–9
Buehlen, Emma, 82–83
Buerstatte, Marian, 82
Buffum, H., 137
Burford, Dick, 65
Burford, Harrie, 137
Burnett, Alma, 66
Buschini, Carl, 117
Buschini, Mrs., 117
Buschini, Pearl, 117
Bussell, Mary Morris, 108–9
Bussini, Mrs., 117

Cameron, Sandy, 108–9
Campbell, Arthur A., 61
Campbell, Bernie, 66
Campbell, Martin, 108–9
Cannon, Mildred, 82
Canutt, Yakama, 138
Caris, Mathias A., 108–9
Carters, Edwin, 66
Casey, George, 92
Casey, John, 85
Casey, Tom, 85
Caston, Donald, 82
Cavelier, Pearl, 65
celebration, about, 135
Chamberling, Louise, 65
Chapman, Esther, 82–83
City Brewery, 8
Clem Bergevin Ranch, 31
Clodius, Henry, 114
Coleman, W.G. "Bill," 68
College Place, 17, 65, 69, 82
Colley, Ben, 120

Colley, Nadine, 82
commerce & industry, about, 43
Conlan, J.R., 92
Cookerly, Grova C., 69
Cookerly, Mattie Coleman, 116
Cooper, Dr., 63
Copeland, Laura, 65
Corkrum, Othel, 66
Coryell, Madeline Cookerly, 116
Cote, Agnes and Clinton, 157
Cote, Annette, 157
County Auditor's office, 87
Crampton, Ralph, 82
Crawford, James T., 61
Crawford, J.M., and family, 37
Crawford, John M., 61
Crawford, Lucille, 82–83
Crayne, Bethene, 67
Crites, Lester, 61
Cropp, Hallie, 65
Croue, Mrs., 63
Cummings, Joseph, children of, 106
Cummings, Sheik, 152
Cummins, Amos, 108–9
Cummins, Clarence, 150
Cummins, Johny, 150
Cummins, Woodson, 108–9
Cunningham, Ed, 137
Cunningham, J.H., 61
Cunnington, Francis, 152
Cunnington, Jake, 152
Cunnington, Mr., 81
Curcio, Emily Jean, 82
Curcio, Mike, 144
Curcio, Rose, 74

Damese family, 105
Danielson, Blanche, 153
Danielson, Ralph, 153
Darch, John, 82
Darling, Leo, 21
Darron, Mark, 65
Davidson, "Tuffy," 29
Davin, Armand, 152
Davis, Irene Gilkerson, 153

Davis, Thomas, 21
Davis, Wallace, 147
Dayton, 8, 130
Dayton Courthouse, 93
Delaney, Bert, 68
Dewitt, America, 108–9
Dewitt, Ob, 108–9
Dimick, Mr., 81
disasters, about, 125
Dixie Elementary School, 80
Dodd, Mildred, 82–83
Doll, Harold, 147
Doroty, Tom, 85
Dotson, Joybelle, 82
Draper, Ella, 45
Draper, Maggie, 45
Draper, William and Margaret, 101
Drumheller, Oscar, 61
Duelley, Verna, 65
Dunn, Junior, 82
Dusenberry, Carl, 137

education, about, 63
Emigh, Ed, 68
Estes, Myrtle, 65
Evans, Andrew J., 108–9
Evans, George, 108–9
Evans, Lena, 65
Evans, Milton, 108–9

Fagg, Aaron "Buck," 29
Fagg, Boyd, 29
Fazzari, Louie, 59
Fehlberg, Ernie, 28
Ferndale School, 80
Ferrel, Genevieve Gilkerson, 153
Fix, Arminda L., 67
Fleenor, Gladys, 119
Fleenor, Madge, 119
Fletcher, Pauline, 82
Fogarty, Doris, 82–83
Fore, Oran, 31
Forrest, Elmer, 29
Forrest, John, 29
Forrest, Melvin, 29

Forrest, Velma, 29
Fort Walla Walla, 87, 92, 95
Fouts, Mr., 81
Frank, Emmanuel, and family, 121
Frasier, Cantrell, 108–9
Freewater, Oregon, 26, 143
Fritsche, Helen, 82
Froenske, Donald, 147

Galbraith, Lacey, 68
Gardner, Shirley, 116
Gardner, Tommy, 152
Gentry, Alice, 67
Giana sisters, 116
Gilbert, Henry, Jr., 73
Gilham, Archie, 68
Gilkerson, Lee, 153
Gilkerson, Ruth, 153
Goldman, Camille, 65
Goodman, Deane, 106
Goodman, Irene Stewart, 101
Goodman, Myrtle, 101
Goodman, Wm. S. "Billy," 101, 105–6
Goodwin, L.C., 92
Gorman, D.M., 48
Gorman, J.E., 48
Grant, Elda, 76
Grant, Sam, 76
Grassi, Eleanor, 82
Gray, George, 68
Greene, Orva, 67
Green Park School, 71, 73, 82
Gregory, Carl, 94
Gregory, Charles, 108–9
Griffith, Elva, 66
Groom, M.P., and family, 99
Grosse, Ruby, 78–79
Guthridge, George, 94

Haggerty, Thomas, 74
Haines, Janell, 82
Ham, Albert, 76
Ham, Dollie, 76
Ham, Melvin, 76
Hammond, Mr. and Mrs., 143
Hansen, Audley, 32–33
Hansen, Hans, 74
Hansen, Hans "Pete," 66
Hanson, Audby, 150
Hanson, Hayden, 150
Hanson, Preston, 150

Harbert, Frank, 108–9
Harbert, Jo S., 108–9
Harding, Bob and Hazel, 119
Harmon, Gladys, 82–83
Harris, Art, 143
Hart, Tom, 89
Hartley, Robert, 82
Hastings, Glen, 82–83
Hauerbach, Otto A., 63
Hawkins, Wanda, 82
Hawley, Will, 108–9
Hector, Mildred, 82
Henchaw, Miss, 80
Hendrick, Charles, 68
Hennesy, Mr, 85
Hill, Shirley, 116
Hines, Miss, 74
Hooper, 29
Hooper, Dallas A., 29
Hottel, Martha Jane, 147
Howard, Lester, 82
Huie, Faye, and children, 123
Huie, Jim, 123
Hungate, Mr. and Mrs. H. H., 108–9
Hunt, Elbert, 74
Huntington, B.M., 61
Hussey, Verla, 66

Ivy, Anne Caldwell, 104

Jackson, Dola, 143
Jackson, Edna, 41, 114
Jackson, Frank, 41, 114, 119
Jackson, Ginger, 123
Jackson, Harold and Gertie, 41
Jackson, Jack, 41, 123
Jackson, Rachel, 41
Jackson, Ralph, 41, 154
Jacobs, Jean, 82
Jaussaud, Leon, 27
Jaussaud, Leon, and family, 117
Jaycox, Hazel, 65
Jefferson School, 80
Jeffery, Henry, 108–9
Jensen, Eva, 74
Jensen, Grace, 82
Jermino, Joe, 25
Johnson, Araid, 82
Johnson, Margaret, 147
Johnson, William, 108–9
Jones, Bob, 43
Jones, D.V., 74

Jones, F. Lowden, 61
Jones, George W., 43
Jordan, J.S., 108–9
Judge, Ray, 21

Kain, Barbara, 82
Kalisky, Joseph, 147
Kauffman, Jack, 92
Kauffman, Jake, 85
Kelley, John G., 61
Kelly, Ginger Jackson, 41
Kelso, Mabel, 67
Kennedy, R., 108–9
Kenney, Jack, 82
Kerr, Jay, 82
Kibler, Robert, 29, 80
Kimball, Judd, 74
Kimbell, Wm. H., 137
King, Caroline Zaro, 117
Kyger, Dan, 48

LaClair, Dan, 152
Laman, Mr., 81
Lammers, Evelyn, 74
Lamnero, Evelyn, 66
Lane, C.B., 56
LaRue, Jerry, 82
La Salle School, 72, 74
Leachris, Nels, 150
Lehman, Sherman, 82
LeRoux, Bud, 74
Lester, Clyde, 61
Lewis Peak Schoolhouse, 73
Liberty Pool Hall, 60
Lincoln School, 79
Linrud, Thora, 82–83
Lloyd, A.J., 108–9
Lloyd, Tony, 113
Lloyd, Wesley, 113
Locati, Ambrosina, 117
Locati, Fred, 117
Locati, Giuseppe, 23, 117
Locati, James, 117
Locati, Josephine, 117
Locati, Lawrance, 82
Locati, Pierina Mainini, 117
Locati, Remo, 117
Locati, Tony, 144
Lockhart, Mr., 81
Loiacono, Dominic, 61
Loiseau, Lannes, 74
Long, Mr., 29

Lonneker, Matilda, 52
Loomis, Miss, 63
Loucks, Andrew, 41
Lovell, Earl, 150
Lowden, 12, 49, 105
Lowden, Frank, Sr., 108–9
Lucinger, J.J. "Jake," 123
Lyman, W.D., 63, 108–9
Lynch, Mary Robison, 30–31, 121

Magnaghi, Frank, 82
Maiden, C.C., 108–9
Manuel, Geraldine, 82
Manuel, Johnny, 82
Margan, McAllister Lanna, 108–9
Marmes, Joe, 29
Marsh, Dorey, 66
Marsh, Dorsey, 74
Marshall, Houston, 66
Martin, Betty Sue, 82
Martin, Chas., 143
Masey, Jack, 143
Matthews, Dana, 116
Maxwell, Estelle, 82
May, Edna, 66
McAuliff, James, 89
McCauley, Doris, 82
McDaniels, Mr., 81
McDonnell, Joseph, and family, 102
McDonnell, Joseph and Alicia, 104
McFaden, Clyde H., 110
McFaden, D. W., 37, 48
McKean, Charles, 88, 143
McKee, Mrs. Phelinda, 108–9
McKinzie, I.A., 92
McLean, Eleanor, 115, 147
McLean, Gordon, 115
McLean, Margery, 115
McLeod, Tex, 138
Meeker, Ezra, 138–39
Merry, F.R., 98–99
Merry, John, 25, 98–99
Merry, Louisa, 98–99
Messenger, Earl, 76
Metz, Bill, 85
Miller, Christina, 82
Miller, Margaret, 106
Miller, May, 65
Miller, Mr., 81
Miller, Norman, 82
Mills, G.W., 137
Milton-Freewater, 80, 148–49, 153

Minnick, Clifford, 68
Mitchell, Dave, 61
Mitchell, Fred, 120
Moffet, Edith, 65
Mohrland, Henry, 31
Money, Jack and Ethel, 41
Montgomery, Charles, 82
Moore School, 66
Moro, Ben, 31
Morton, J., 82–83
Moulton, Lois, 82
Mud Creek railway wreck, 125
Mudhy, Marion, 150

Natatorium, Walla Walla, 150
National Guard, 89, 95, 150
Native Americans, 87, 113, 146–47
Nayes, Thelma M., 82
Nesbin, Samuel, 147
Nixon, Art, 106
Nixon, Edward H., 106
Nixon, Laura, 106
Noland, Roy, 66
Nuttall, Will, 108–9

O'Brien, Patrick M., 117
Ogden, Lila, 82
O'Hair, Brownie, 152
Olson, Laura P., 82
Onriegs, Forest, 147
Onstot, Mr., 81
Oregon Railroad and Navigation Co., 34
Oregon–Washington Railroad and Navigation Co., 33, 127
Otta, Loche Van, 82
Owsley, Kenneth, 152

Paine, Frank, 86
Paine School, 64
Palrick, Marge, 66
Papoon, Helen A., 63
Parker, Charles, 154
Parker, Hollon, 108–9
Parker, Stella, 154
Pasco Sam, 113
Paul School House, 76
Penrose, Dr., 63
people, about, 99
Perrin, Henry, 92
Peterson, N.D., 92
Pettijohn, Louise, 82–83

Walla Walla Valley Memories

Pettyjohn, Lawerence, 76
Pettyjohn School, 76
Phillips, Chas. W., and children, 137
Pickard, Tom, 85
Pioneer Association, 108–9, 147
Pioneer Grocery, 45
Plumber's Union, 59
Pomeroy, 57
Pope, Edith, 82
Poplar Grove School, 69
Porter, Mr., 81
Powers, Dorothy, 66
Pratt, Virginia, 82
Prescott, 9, 76
Prescott School, 72
Preston, Dale, 54–55
public service, about, 85

Ramsey, Eliza, 67
Ray, Goldie, 76
Ray, Ivory, 76
Ray, Myrtle, 76
Ray, Wanda, 76
recreation, about, 135
Reely, Walter, 82
Reeves, Mark W., 137
Reid, Bill, 115
Reid, Eunice, 108, 115
Reid, Gladys, 108
Rice, Nancy E., 108–9
Rich, Teddy, 82
Richmond, Earl, 66
Ringel, Elsa, 21
Ringel, Emma, 21
Ringel family reunion, 107
Ritz, Mrs. Philip, 108–9
Robberson, Arline, 147
Robberson, Clayton, 82
Robberson, Elva, 147
Robinson, Richard, 82
Rohn, J.J., 108–9
Rorke, Jack and Mary, 103
Rup, Rudolph, 68
Rupp, Irma, 67
Russel, Bobby, 82
Russel, Edith L., 82
Russell, Lenore, 82
Ryan, John "Jack," 100
Ryan, Mary Gavin, 100
Ryger, Tat, 65

Sama, Elmer, 82

Saturno, Carmen, 39
Saturno, Josephine, 25
Saturno, Pasquale, 25
Saturno family, 111
Saxt, Gene, 116
Saxton, Don, 116
Saxton, Ruth, 116
Scheece, Eleanor, 82
Schmeltzer, June, 82
Schneller, Lorraine, 74
Schole, Mrs. and Mrs. Louis, 108–9
schools, about, 63
Schubert, Jacob, 46
Schwarz, Adolph, Jr., 110–11
Schwarz, Ruth, 111
Scott, Jap and Mrs., 108–9
Sharp, Arita, 76
Sharpstein School, 73–74
Shaw, Clarence and Bessie, 121
Shelton, Laura, 108–9
Sherry, James Wallace, 24
Shortridge, Earl, 27
Smith, Bert, 154
Smith, Cecil, 120
Smith, Charles, 120
Smith, Cy, 106
Smith, Elmer, 31
Smith, Frances, 82
Smith, Geo., children of, 122
Smith, Geo. W., 31, 120
Smith, Ted, 31
Smith, Vasco, 143
Smutten, Ednid, 65
Snyder, Guenn, 108
Snyder, Henry, 29
Snyder, John M.P., 108
Snyder, Tess, 65
Spanish, Agnes Zaro, 117
St. Mary's Nursing School, 80
St. Patrick's School, 66
St. Paul's School, 65
St. Vincent Academy, 68, 81
Stafford, Mr., 70–71
Starbuck, 13
Starrett, Mrs. George, 108–9
State Penetentiary, 86, 90–91, 148
Statsman, Howard, 66
Steward, Loren, 147
Stewart, Albert, 68
Stewart, Bob, 106
Stewart, Charles, 101, 106
Stewart, Crass, 106

Stewart, Daniel, 106
Stewart, Etta, 106
Stewart, Kate Day, 106
Stewart, Loretta Belle, 101
Stewart, Mamie, 106
Stimmel, Lila, 82
Stimmel, Orval, 82
Stine, Helen, 82
Stirling, Marjorie, 147
Stockdale, Howard, 152
Stone, Edna, 65
Stoover, Patricia, 82
Sturm, Rita, 66
Suckow, Otto E., 28
Summers, Howard, 152
Summers, Jean, 147
Summers, John, 152
Summers, Robert, 152
Sutherland, Ray, 68
Swegle, Barbara, 82
Switzler, Eva, 65

Taft, William Howard, 141
Tarwater, Curtis, 116
Tarwater, Virginia, 116
Task, Cliff, 153
Tausick, Eugene, 61
Taylor, Anne, 65
Taylor, Esther, 116
Taylor, Jessie, 116
Teal, Bobby, 82
Teal, Cyrus H., 52
Thomas, Bert, 63
Thomas, Eloise, 82
Thomas, Gilbert, 153
Thomas, Isabell, 82
Thomas, Melissa, 67
Thompson, Gaylord, 66
Thompson, George, 68
Tighe, Dessie, 66
Timmons, John H., 40
Todorovich, John, 82
Tompkins, Charles A., and family, 111
Touchet, 46, 142–43, 153
Touchet High School, 71
Touchet River, 24
train wrecks, 125, 127
transportation, about, 33
Tricks, Lydia, 119
Trimble, Evelyn, 74
Tuttle, John C., 116

Union Pacific Railroad station, 34
Utter, Charlotte, 76

Vahe, Elizabeth, 82
Vail, Geraldine, 82
VanDeWater, Wm., 143
Veterans' Administration Hospital, 97
Vietz, Arlene, 82
views, about, 7
Villa, Mrs. Frank, 108–9

Wacker, Jake, 82
Waitsburg, 21, 23, 54–55, 141
Waitsburg Academy, 64
Waldron, E.L., 49
Walla Walla
    buildings, 6–7, 37, 39, 45, 48, 56, 59, 92–93, 126, 145
    businesses, 12, 43–44, 46, 48–52, 56–57, 59–61, 95, 127, 151
    celebrations and parades, 34, 44, 134–36, 138–41, 144–47, 150–51, 154, 157
    churches, 78–79, 94, 148
    dining and accommodations, 12, 35–36, 44–45, 47, 53, 59
    fire department, 85–87, 89, 91, 94–95
    fires and floods, 124–27, 130–33
    hospitals, 53, 56
    people of, 12, 25, 42–44, 51–52, 78–79, 85–87, 108, 153, 155
    police department, 92, 96
    railway depot, 35
    ranches, farms, and orchards, 20, 26–31
    scenes of, 7–17, 35, 37, 127–29, 144
    symphony and orchestra, 154
Walla Walla College, 69
Walla Walla High School, 68–69, 74–75, 77, 81
Walla Walla Symphony and Orchestra, 154
Wallula ferry, 39
Wallula School, 64
Warren, Atta Marie, 147
Washington School, 70–72, 81
Wasser, Bobby, 82

Watkins, Aileen, 82
Weathers, Anna, 143
Weathers, Dolph, 143
Weathers, Jesse, 143
Weathers, Lou, 143
Webb, Helen, 82, 118
Webb, Mary Jane, 118
Webb, Minta Pettyjohn, 118
Webb, Mollie Valaer, 106
Webb, Nat, 108–9
Webb, Nat, Jr., 106
Webb, Paul, Jr., 118
Webb, Paul, Sr., 106, 117–18
Webb, Ruth, 118
Weir, Harry, 48
Welch, Nadine, 65
Wellman, A.C., 108–9
Wetzel, Claude, 152
Wheeler, Mr., 54–55
Whitman College, 63, 65–67, 76–77, 147
Whitman Eells Memorial Church, 8
Williams, T.A., 61
Wilson, Mayme, 104
Winans, Elmer R., 106
Winans, Ida, 106
Winans, William P., 112–13
Winchell, Buck, 150
Witt, Francis, 152
Witt, Philander, 108–9
Wolf, Robert J., funeral, 85
Wood, D.V., 56
Wood, Robert, 56
Woods, Walter, 54–55

Yelle, Mollie and Nazaire, 120
Yelley, Harv, 40
Yenney, John, 115
YMCA, 151
York, Dillard, 148–49
York, Grant, 148–49
York, Guy, 143
York, Jess, 148–49
York, Ranzy, 148–49
Young, Blanche, 65
Young, Chesel, 66
Young, Fred, 137
Young, Harlan, 21

Zaro, Charles, 117
Zaro, Giovinna, 117
Zaro, Joe, 117